THE A TO Z

BOOK OF

GODS

By Michael P. Earney

Copyright Michael P. Earney 2021 All Rights Reserved.
No part of this book may be reproduced, stored in a retrieval system, or transmitted by any means, electronic, mechanical, photocopying, recording, or otherwise, without written permission from the author.

ISBN-13:   978-1-941345-91-7   HB
ISBN-13:   978-1-941345-92-4   PB

Cover design by Michael P. Earney

The Sun God Aton shines in the blue heaven. The Ankh, Egyptian symbol of life is behind the staff of Mercury, messenger of the gods. The hand of god reaches out to give life to Adam, as depicted on the ceiling of the Sistine chapel by Michelangelo.

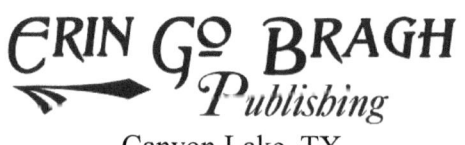

Canyon Lake, TX
www.ErinGoBraghPublishing.com

Ye Gods!

Do the gods of Olympus still look down from on high?

Does the kitchen god still preside when we fry?

They are all around us, one for this, one for that

for the doorway, for the hearth, even one for the cat.

A Lord of the Thunder, a Lord of the Rain

Is that a god flying? No it's only a crane.

Still, they do come along in a number of guises

so you need to be ready for any surprises.

With so many gods to adore and placate

that one simple slip-up could seal your fate.

You must have faith and say all of your prayers

That way, in the end, you may go "upstairs"

And, if at last you get to the "Heavenly Gate"

Have your answers all ready, St. Peter can't wait

There are plenty of souls being placed on the scales,

those that spoke wrongly, that sound is their wails

as they head for the fire and brimstone below,

The place where, believe me, you don't want to go.

There are plenty of choices, so, that's the good news

just hope that your loved ones go along with your views.

M. P. Earney Dec. 2020

Acknowledgements

Thanks to Barbara Baggett for her editorial work.
Thanks to the North Family.
And a special thank you to Kathleen J. Shields for her
tireless work bringing the book to completion.

Disclaimer

Every effort has been made to trace the copyright holders
and we apologize in advance for any unintentional omissions.
We would be pleased to insert the appropriate acknowledgment
in any subsequent editions of this publication.

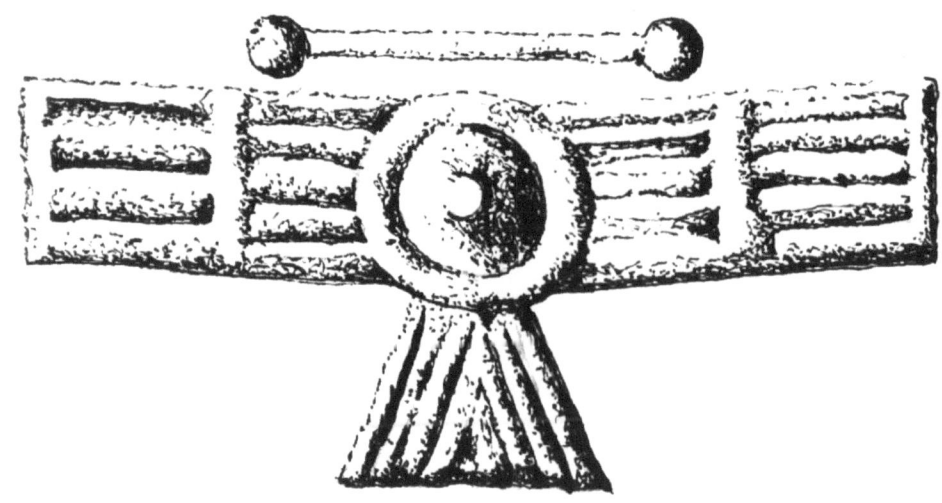

Introduction

Are we, as countless religious texts, creation stories and ancient depictions tell, an invention of the gods, or are we the inventors of the gods? The Sumerians who occupied the Tigris, Euphrates delta for thousands of years, inventing the wheel, writing, and agriculture using large irrigation systems, building great cities ruled by kings who were said to have lived for thousands of years and claimed to have been created by the Anunaki, beings that came down from the heavens. It was later generations that called those beings gods. Some religions have the gods creating the earth first, the creation of mankind coming as an afterthought. Such tales may have evolved from cave-dwellers' long nights gathered around the fire telling stories. Perhaps, as so often happens, the recounting of an actual event was embellished with a little exaggeration; Billy caught a fish, was it really six feet long though, and you spent three days in the belly of a whale, is that right, Jonah? Through thousands of years more stories came, were expanded upon, morphed into accepted fact handed down from generation to generation, spreading from tribe to tribe. Story telling became an art practiced by schools of bards. Tales that might take a week or more to unfold had to be committed to memory, often accompanied by music and sometimes sung. Theater and pageantry brought more power and magic to messages being delivered. Young, impressionable minds are shaped by the stories heard and never forgotten. As Mankind spread across the globe, these stories went with them, tales of gods gave birth to religion, morality tales, rules and laws. Fairies and goblins, mythical beasts all were out there in those realms unexplored and unknowable. It was to the gods that any inexplicable phenomena was attributed. The succession of night and day, the seasons, the sky above; all were studied and explanations sought. Many blind alleys were followed and the search for answers goes on. Once worshiped as gods and goddesses, the sun and the moon, (in some beliefs the sun was a god, the moon a goddess, in others it was the other way round) we now know are part of our planetary system. The Milky Way once seen as the gateway to the heavens, a path to immortality, is seen now as a galaxy of which the earth is but a part. The universe, still largely unknown, may yet offer answers or like our planet, come up with even more questions. The fact of the matter is that it would seem gods have inhabited the earth for as long as mankind or, as many peoples have told, for longer. As the great civilizations of the Near and Far East came into being and faded away, the lands to the north, Europe, Russia, Scandinavia, England and Ireland were populated by hunter/gatherers and tribes living in small settlements, each worshiping their gods and goddesses of nature in sacred groves, at holy springs and sacrificial altars. "Knowledge Keepers" rather than priests unified the tribes, no one religion prevailed over another until Christianity was introduced. Though there may be less gods today there are still plenty of religions, some that include a deity, others that do not. Hinduism, Islam, Christianity and Buddhism, along with lesser-known religions that have been practiced for centuries are still being observed, while new ones are gaining followers. Pastafarianism, ruled by the Flying Spaghetti Monster, has some 10 million followers observing the tenets of, "niceness and good behavior among all beings." Without judging the veracity or plausibility of any of the beliefs surrounding the gods examined, we will look at them in the context of history and their place in the lives of those that worshiped them. Dating back to the earliest times religion has been the greatest inspiration to artists in every medium through the ages to this day. Temples, statuary, images of every kind produced prior to the introduction of writing remain as evidence for the existence of gods. Architectural and artistic masterpieces that have stood the test of time still amaze and delight the viewer or listener. Religion promoted learning and skills that would add to the lives of believers. It inspires goodness and kindness in its devotees, it has also brought out the worst kind of destruction, murder, and mayhem in the name of its lord. From the Sumerians, the Akkadians, Egyptians, Hebrews, Greeks, and Romans we have records of their gods instigating and actively participating in the wars of their people. A variation on that is when the Spanish were driving the Moors out of Spain; Saint James appeared on the battlefield at a crucial time leading to Spain's success. "Santiago!" (St. James) became the battle cry when, shortly thereafter, Spain invaded the Americas and the Spanish were forced to subdue the natives there, confident that God was on their side.

Worldwide, death and destruction on behalf of and abetted by the gods appears to have been the norm forever, not that mankind isn't capable of such action unaided. Still, it does beg the question, if God is good, how come all the death and destruction?

The loss of, and deliberate destruction of libraries throughout the thousands of years has robbed us of much of the early histories of China and India. *The Mahabharata,* an Indian epic, tells of earlier wars when a priest-king, despite saying, "We of India do not believe in war and strife, peace being our ideal" was compelled to fight off his enemies. The epic has a description of the outcome, here are the verses:

"Gurkha, flying a swift and powerful vimana,
hurled a single projectile
charged with all the power of the universe.
An incandescent column of smoke and flame,
as bright as ten thousand suns, rose with all its splendor.

It was an unknown weapon, an iron thunderbolt,
a gigantic messenger of death, which reduced to ashes
the entire race of the Vrishnis and the Andhakas.

China, being so vast, had hundreds of gods, mostly nature deities, six creation stories, in one an incestuous relationship between a brother and sister brings about human beings, four flood stories that did not involve retribution from on high and, again perhaps due to its size, no nationwide religion. Confucianism, while it did become an institutionalized religion, did not include gods. Similarly, Taoism was a philosophical school of thought before it, briefly, became a religion. Buddhism, imported from India, like Taoism, had its temples and priesthoods, no gods involved, however.

India nurtured thousands of gods, the many dating from the earliest times being augmented by those brought in with the Aryan invaders around 1500BCE although no national religion arose until Hinduism absorbed many of them. Hinduism, the third-largest religion in the world, coexists along with its offshoots, Buddhism and Jainism, carrying on a less easy relationship with Islam that rules most of the Middle East.

The continent of Africa, accepted as the cradle of mankind, having millions of years start on everywhere else, supported a supreme god together with countless nature gods and goddesses, demigods, tricksters, spirits, and otherworldly souls influencing every aspect of life. While Christianity and Islam are the main religions today it is estimated that more than 100 million Africans still practice some form of traditional religion. African slaves carried some of those traditions to the New World where native peoples, from the Arctic down to Tierra del Fuego had, over the thousands of years of migration, established belief systems that developed along with mighty empires while still more have remained closely held secrets of the tribes that abide by their tenets.

There are more gods than we can or ever will know, a collection of some from around the world are presented here.

Note: This is not a book about religions, religions form around the god, ruler, lord, leader, prophet or chosen one representing the "received knowledge" which, once it is put out into the world is open to interpretation, revision and mutation. Scholars and those claiming to have been given the true knowledge of the faith, give "the word of god" their own determination that then becomes, for its followers, the only truth. The faithful have been led into endless warring and discrimination between the branches and sects within the sects, all requiring total adherence to their call and rejection of any that disagree with one or other versions of "The Truth." Centuries of race pitted against race, gender against gender, nations warring against nations, families torn apart in an endless cycle of hatred and killing, all in the name of god.

> When we blindly adopt a religion,
> a political system, a literary dogma,
> we become automatons. We cease to grow.
> -Anaïs Nin

A IS FOR ATON, ATEN. ATONU, ITN

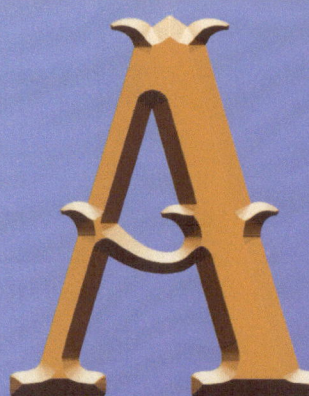

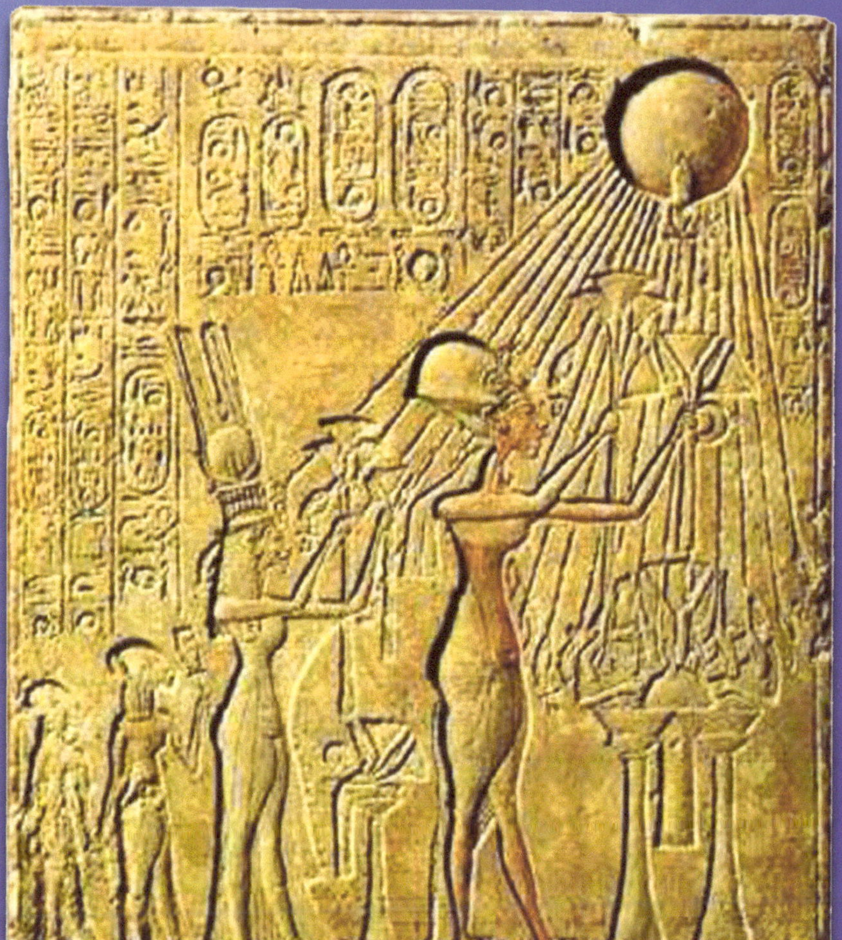

Aton, the sun god, was favored by Amenhotep III even though, as Pharoah, he represented the sun god Amon-Re. His son, Amenhotep IV, shortly after succeeded to the throne, decided that henceforth, Aton would be the supreme god and set about erasing references to all the other gods. This did not please the priests, generals and other officials whose careers were tied to the worship of Amon-Re. The ancient god Re, who had created himself and eight other gods, had evolved into Amon-Re and for more than a millennium was the "King of the Gods." Erasing that much establishment would be an uphill battle. Amenhotep ("Amon is content") changed his name to Akhnaton ("beneficial to Aton"), and built an impressive new capital two hundred miles away from Thebes, where Amon-Re was worshiped. There the temples were open to the sky so that Aton could watch over his people and be worshiped, not as a being but as sunlight and energy itself; later, even representations of the sun disk were prohibited by Akhnaton leaving the actual sun as god. Akhnaton was innovative in many other ways, he and his family were portrayed realistically rather than as iconic figures, all the usual activities of worship were stripped down, leaving priests with little to do.

An Aton hymn:

Men had slept like the dead; now they lift their arms in praise, birds fly, plants bloom, and work begins. Aton creates the son in his mother's womb, the seed in men, and has generated all life. He has distinguished the races, their natures, tongues and skins, and fulfills the needs of all. Aton made the Nile in Egypt and rain, like a heavenly Nile, in foreign countries. He has one million forms according to the time of day and from where he is seen: yet he is always the same.

Atonism has been cited as the first example of monotheism but, Akhnaton did not deny the existence of other gods; he required that only Aton be worshiped. In fact the Pharoah himself was considered a god; divine revelation being reserved for him alone, and while he and his wife Nefertiti, worshiped Aton together, the people worshiped him. With so little in the way of dogma for the people to observe, it's very likely that the majority of Egyptians were unaware that this major change had taken place. The Amarna period, as it is known, only lasted from 1353-1336BC. After succeeding his father at the age of eight or nine, Tutenkhaten, no doubt under the influence of his vizier and cabinet, chose to reverse all of his father's innovations; changing his name to Tutankhamon, moving the capital back to Thebes, restoring the temples of Amon and desecrating those of Aton. A sickly child, Tutenkhamon was afflicted by many ailments, perhaps due in part to inbreeding; his mother may have been his father's sister, he also suffered from malaria. He reigned for nine years, his death brought an end to the 18th Dynasty that had lasted for 200 years.

Cool Fact: Nefertiti may have outlived Akhnaton but mystery and speculation surround her history after that event. Her tomb has never been found, it's possible that those who tried to erase the Amarna period also saw to it that nothing remained of her. However, thanks to the famous bust of Nefertiti, attributed to the sculptor Thutmose, which is one of the most copied works of ancient Egypt, she is known world-wide. **What other gods' names start with A?**

B IS FOR BAAL

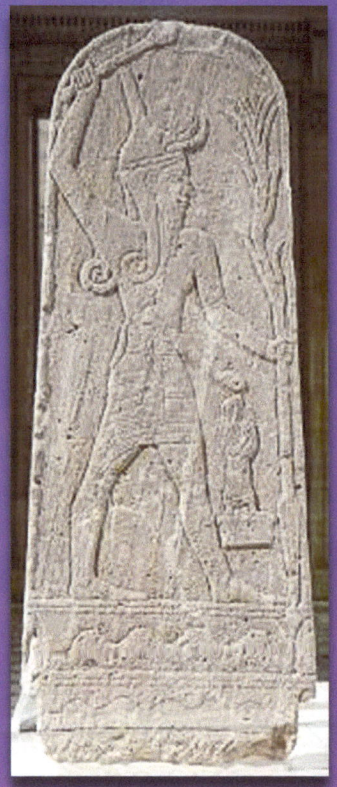
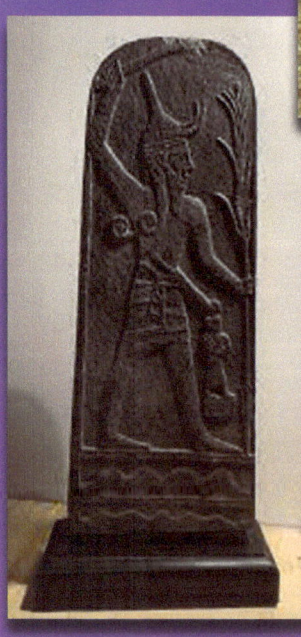
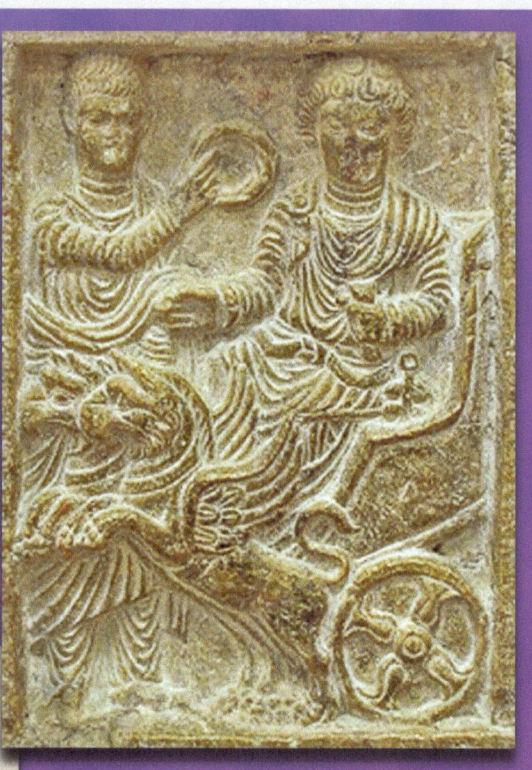

Baal, Ba'al, Universal god of fertility, Lord of the earth, Lord of the Rain and Dew, Lord of the Heavens. Baal worship was popular in Egypt from 1400BCE-1075BCE and throughout the Middle East but Canaan, an arid area, was the base for Baal's worship as the god of fertility where there was a great dependency on rain for crops. Occupied from at least 8000BCE, Canaan is identified as covering all of Palestine and part of Syria although sometimes only as land west of the Jordan river. The Canaanites are identified in Genesis of the Bible as the descendants of Canaan, a son of Ham and the grandson of Noah. At the ancient ruins of Ugarit in Syria there is a temple to Baal Shamen, Lord of the Heavens. Most of our knowledge of Baal comes from tablets uncovered in 1929 in N. Syria. As god of life and fertility he was locked in combat with Mot, god of death and sterility, if he won there was seven years of fertility if he lost, seven years of drought and famine so, a lot of prayers going out. Baal also sired a divine bull calf from a heifer as part of his fertility role. In addition, Baal was King of the Gods, having seized the divine kingship from Yamm the sea god. Here's where it gets complicated. Baal meant, "Lord" so we see Baal Hadad, Baal Dagan and, as previously mentioned, Baal Shamen. Baal could also be used as a common noun, Ba'al in Hebrew could mean "owner" or "lord." DNA evidence now suggests that the Hebrews branched out from the other Canaanite tribes to establish a different identity. This might explain why Moses led his people out of Egypt to Canaan as their promised land. Since Baal was used liberally to refer to local deities, it wasn't a problem for those early Hebrews to use Baal when referring to their god, Yahweh. In the nineteenth century BCE when Jezebel, a Phoenician, married the Hebrew King Ahab, she continued to worship Baal, as was her right, introducing a kind of polytheism. This didn't sit well with Yahweh who complained to the prophet Elijah leading him to challenge 450 of Baal's priests to a contest; whichever god would send down fire from heaven when called upon, would be declared the true god. Baal's priests couldn't pull it off but, Yahweh sent down fire that consumed offerings, the altar, and the surrounding water, just to banish any doubt. As winners, Yahweh's priests put all of Baal's priests to death. It didn't end there, however, after succeeded his father, Anaziah, Jezebel's son, sustained injuries in a fall, he consulted with priests of Baal Zebul as to whether he would survive. Elijah, convinced he had put Baal out of the picture, was incensed, he declared that Anaziah would die quickly. Soldiers, sent to punish Elijah got the "fire raining down from heaven" treatment. Jezebel got the Elijah treatment too, she was thrown out of a palace window and was eaten by dogs. Her name became synonymous with harlot.

Cool Fact: The very name Baal became anathema to the Hebrews becoming identical to "shame," every effort to eliminate the name from the idea of god was undertaken. Ba'al Zebub, in Hebrew became, "Fly Lord" or "Lord of the Flies" sometimes interpreted as a way of calling Baal a pile of dung. Baal Zebub became the way to signify false gods even all the way down to the Protestant Reformation where it was applied to all idols, icons of saints and to the Catholic Church in general. Ultimately it became, Beelzebub, Satan himself.
What other gods' names start with B?

C IS FOR CHAC, CHAAC, CHAAHK

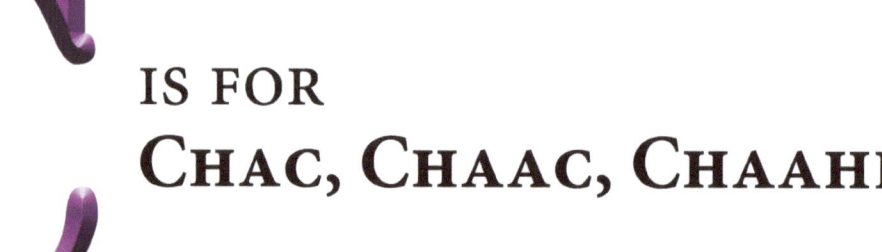

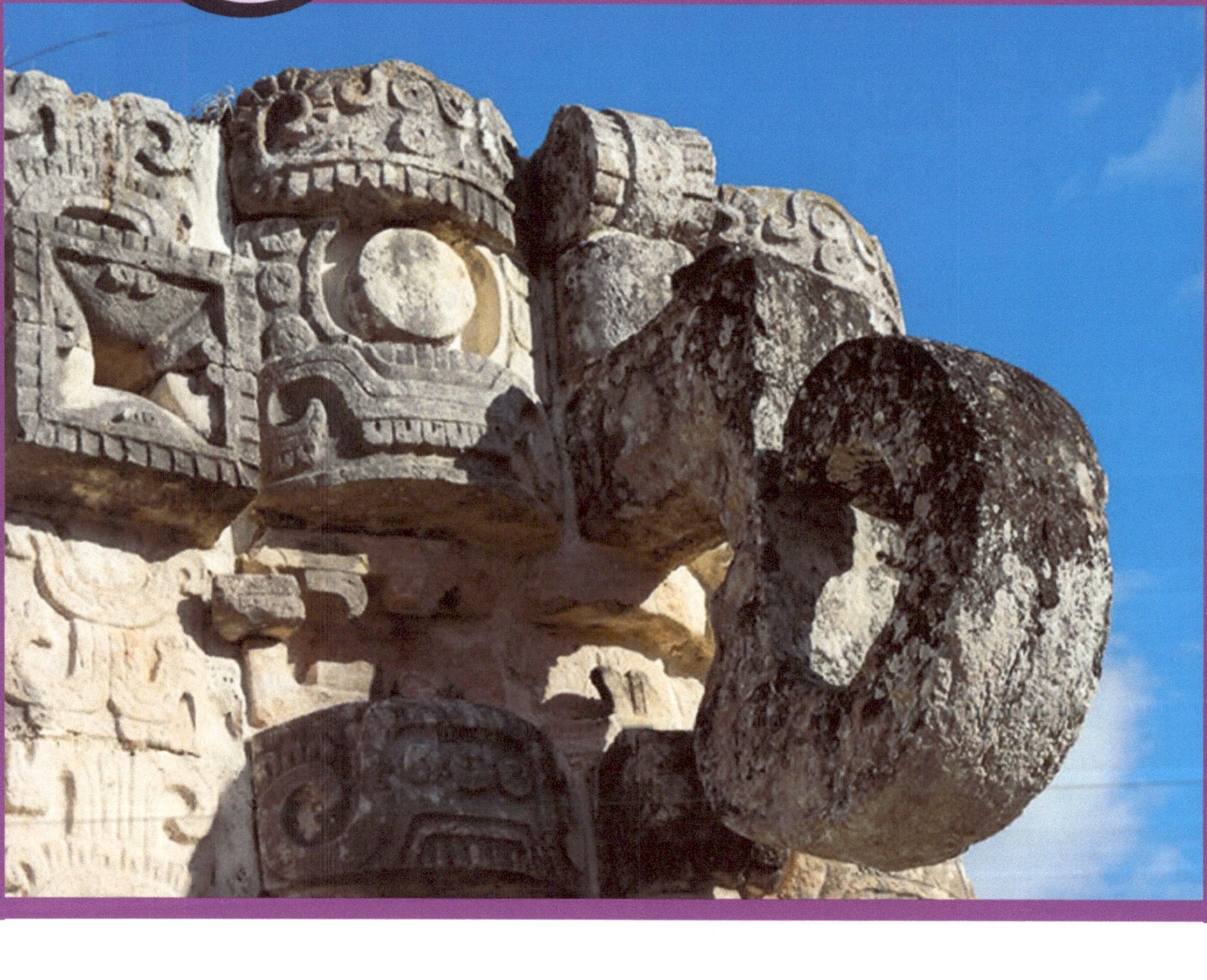

Chac, god of rain and fertility is one of the longest continuously worshiped gods in all of Central America, he is also credited with giving corn to the people by opening a rock that contained the first maize plant; with his lightning axe he strikes the clouds producing thunder and rain. Rain gods figure prominently in the beliefs of agricultural people around the world. The Maya, who occupied a wide variety of ecological niches from the Yucatan to Belize and Guatemala were divided into many tribes and nations with various versions of Chac. The main one was actually four in one, one for each of the cardinal directions, all being a different color. Rain from one direction being quite different from that of another direction. Farmers, those most directly concerned with the weather and its effect on their crops, might have a broader appreciation of rain and clouds, ascribing their formation to yet more gods. As rain deity and patron of agriculture, Chac was of paramount importance to the Maya. Many rituals and ceremonies were undertaken to maintain good relations with Chac and to induce him to provide the much-needed rain at the right time in the right amount. His human counterpart was the rainmaker, this might be a Shaman or the king himself, often being one and the same. Ceremonies in which the rainmaker along with the priests and the people would plead for rain were carried out with passion, dedication, and often, great anxiety. Torture and human sacrifice figured in rainmaking ceremonies. In one a child was placed at each corner of the altar, where they were required to croak like frogs during the proceedings, after which they were sacrificed. In the Yucatan where deep natural wells, known as *cenotes,* formed when part of the limestone rock collapsed, were often the only source of freshwater for much of the year, these too were the sites of prayer and human sacrifice.

Chac was often portrayed as having a human body with scales of a snake or turtle, a non-human head with fangs and a pendulous nose, at times depicted as turned up like an elephant's trunk, carrying a shield and an axe. One myth has Chac being the brother of the sun god Kinich Ahau and that he had an affair with Kinich's wife. Rain that falls is said to be the tears he sheds in regret for what he did. Other stories have Chac not residing in heaven but in caves where sacred water is found.

In 1873 archaeologist Augustus Le Plongeon found a sculpture of a reclining male resting on his elbows, his knees bent, and his head turned to the side holding a bowl or platter on his stomach. Plongeon named the sculpture, Chac Mool, incorrectly thinking it portrayed a Mayan warrior by that name. He was only partly wrong however, more such figures were found throughout Central America and some had inscriptions, a painted Aztec version had figures indicating it was associated with Tlaloc, the Aztec rain god, clearly linking it to rain ceremonies. They evidently served as offering plates where supplicants placed their gifts to the rain god. Mayan communities in the Yucatan continue to hold rain ceremonies, their offerings now include Balche (corn beer); getting drunk had always been part of the rain ceremony

Cool Fact: Carlos Fuentes wrote a short story called, *Chac Mool* in it a young man purchases a replica of a Chac Mool from a junk store. After he gets the sculpture home his water pipes burst and his roof starts to leak rain. With all the moisture the statue comes to life and makes the young man his slave. Then what happens? You'll have to read the story. **What other gods' names start with C?**

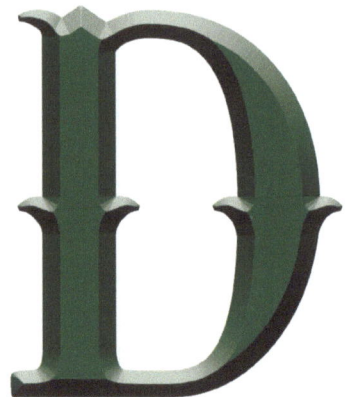

IS FOR
**Dagon,
Dagen**

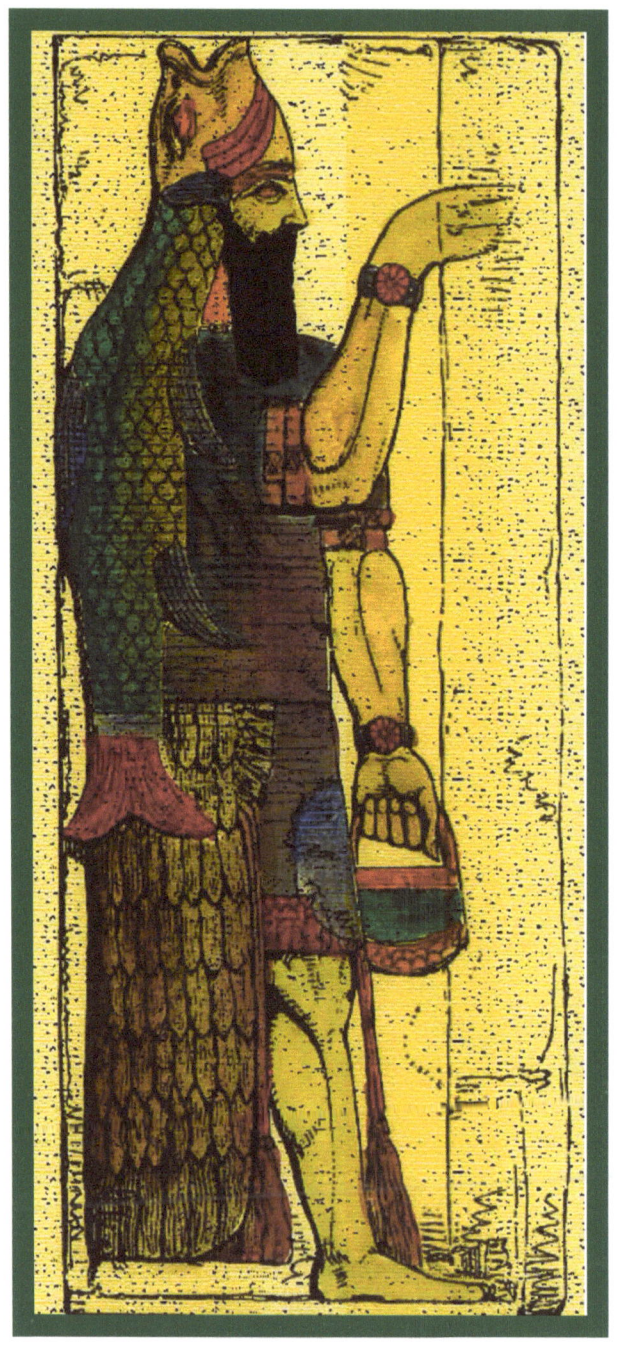

D **agon**, Babylonian god of grain and fertility who also controlled the weather first appeared around 2300 BCE * at Ebla, one of the earliest kingdoms of Syria, where he was head of a pantheon of gods and went under the title of "Lord of the Gods" and "Lord of the Land" in a large temple complex called "House of the Stars," one-quarter of the city was named for him. He was also called "Dew of the land" and was the Lord of many other cities. Early Sumerian texts occasionally mention Dagon but it is in later Assyro-Babylonian texts that he becomes prominent. About a thousand years after his appearance at Ebla, Dagon had a large temple in Ugarit in Northern Syria where he was sometimes equated with El, (elsewhere he is called one of the seventy sons of El) and is best known as the father of Baal. As we have seen, the translation of ancient texts, conflicting accounts, and missing parts of texts, leaves a lot of room for different interpretations, on top of which, there is the fact that El, Baal, Dagon, and many more names meant god or lord and would be added to the name of ordinary people too. Grandiose titles like, "Lord of the Universe" and "Creator of All" were handed out fairly liberally. Still, it is clear he was worshiped extensively over a large part of the Middle East for, just like everywhere else in the world, getting food into the mouths of people was a number one priority. As late as the 4th century CE he is mentioned in the Ethiopian Orthodox Old Testament as a figure of worship even though the Christian Roman Empire had done its best to wipe out Paganism. Strangely, in spite of all the temples, statues, and the prominence of his name, there appears to be little about his role and his place in the hierarchy. All we know is, he was a major god and to some, the chief god.

Cool Fact: Most people are familiar with the story of Samson, thanks in part to Hollywood. After Delilah had seduced him, Samson divulged the source of his strength, his hair. She then turned him over to the Philistines who cut it off. Samson's eyes were gouged out and he was put to work grinding grain in a mill. His hair had grown out again when he was taken to a Philistine temple where he asked to be allowed to rest against one of the pillars supporting the roof. He prayed to God, Yahweh in his case, his strength returned and he pulled down the columns, killing himself and all the Philistines. That temple was dedicated to Dagon, the god of grain.

*2024 BCE was the date given in Zechariah Sitchen's, "The Wars of Gods and Men" that, in his interpretation of the texts from the time, a catastrophic event occurred in the area. He chose to call it a nuclear explosion detonated by the Gods.

What other Gods' names start with D?

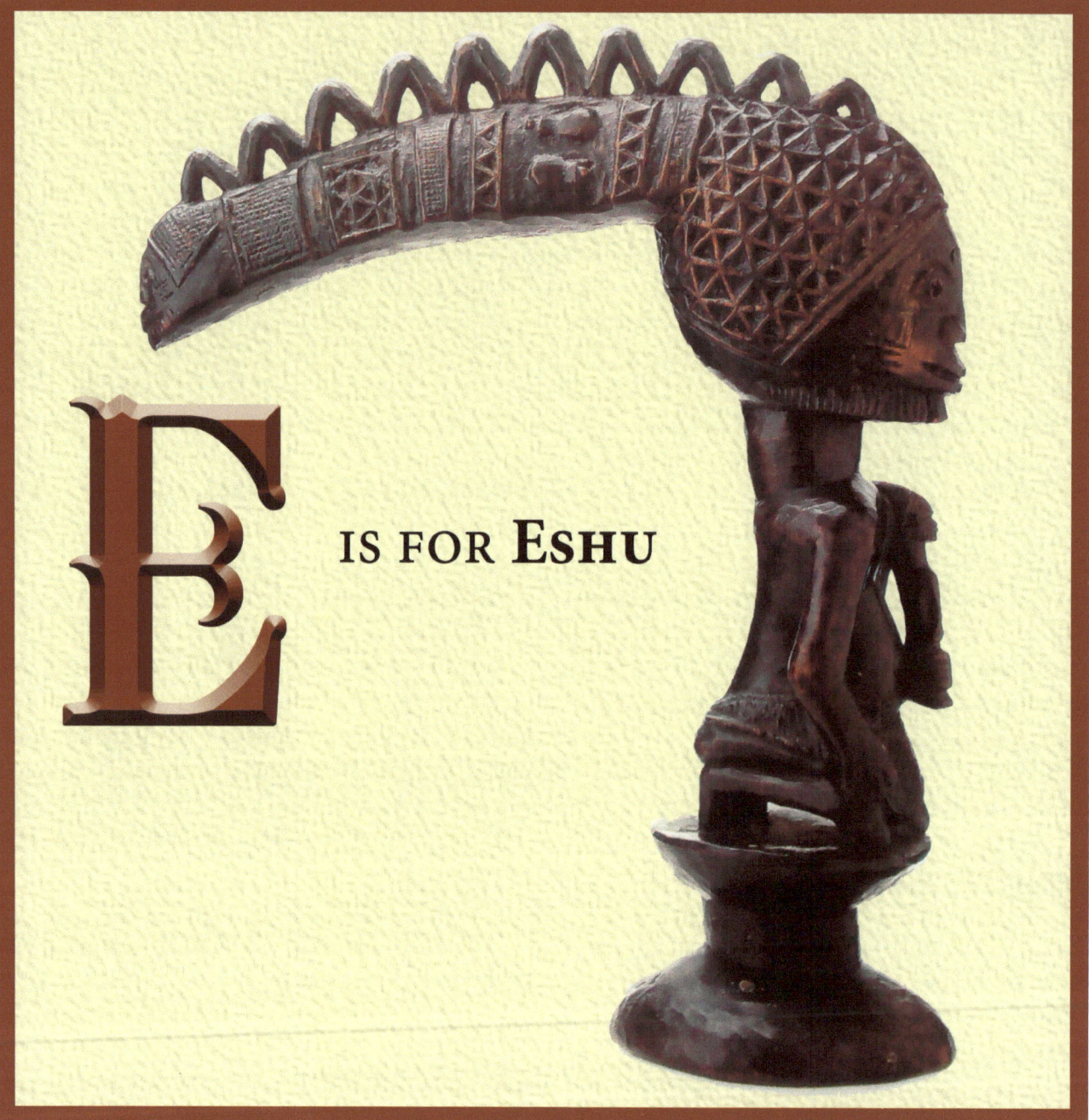

E IS FOR ESHU

Eshu, Echu, Exu. Trickster god of the Yoruba people of West Africa is known by several other names, Legba being the most often used. The Yoruba are one of the three largest ethnic groups in Africa with nearly 40 million people, the area where they live in South West Nigeria is so large that it is referred to as "Yorubaland," another 1.7 million live in Benin and several hundred thousand more live in Ghana and Togo. The Yoruba creation story holds that all Yoruba are descendants of a hero named Odua; only fifty individuals currently claim kingship as descendants from Odua. Some twenty percent of Yoruba still practice the traditional religion. In the beginning, all the gods lived in the sky above the water, the Sun god gave the god of whiteness, Orishala, a chain, a bit of earth, and a five-toed chicken and told him to go down and create the earth. Before leaving, Orishala got drunk with some friends and fell asleep. His younger brother Odua took the items and did the job. Olurun, the sky god, Ifa, the god of divination, and Eshu are the three gods available to all. Eshu became the divine messenger in the following way: after stealing yams from Ifa's garden he used the god's slippers to make footprints in the soil to convince Ifa that he had taken the yams himself. Annoyed, Ifa ordered Eshu to stay awake at night in the sky and tell him what happened on earth each day. He was also tasked with delivering the sacrifices placed on Olurun's shrine to that god. Of the gods, he is one of the most frequently prayed to, as people expect that he will deliver their prays to the appropriate god. He is the protector of travelers and has power over fortune and misfortune. His role as trickster and prankster is to create situations that will become lessons to understanding in a more nuanced and compassionate way, although he is also said to enjoy the strife that can come about as a result of his tricks. Perhaps on the grounds that the harder the lesson the more profound the effect.

Here is one story that has a number of variations: Eshu walked through a village one day wearing a hat that was black on one side and red on the other, setting off arguments between those on opposite sides of the street as to the color of his hat. When the arguments got violent he returned from the other end of the village to show them how one's perspective can lead to closed-mindedness and make a fool of one. How open-mindedness can lead to a more nuanced understanding of reality. The role of the prankster is always to shake us out of a rigid mindset.

"Yorubaland" was known as the Slave Coast of Africa, in the Americas Yoruba communities, descendants of slaves, spread their religion from Cuba, Brazil and beyond: Santeria, a syncretism of Roman Catholicism and Yoruba religion is widely practiced in Cuba where Oshiras (divine messengers) and Ifá figure prominently. Cubans that left after the revolution there, have spread the religion throughout the Americas and to other communities, Latino and White.

Cool Fact: Henry Olusegun Adeolo Samuel, better known as Seal, is Yoruba, born in London, England. He has sold 30 million records worldwide and been a judge on the talent show, The Voice. Discoid lupus erythematosus, DLE, a chronic skin condition that afflicted Seal in his teens, left his cheeks scarred and caused hair loss. Now in remission, the scarring didn't stop him from becoming a world singing star and performer.

What other gods' names start with E?

F

IS FOR
FU HSI,
FU XI,
FUXING

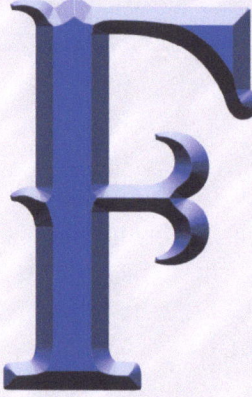

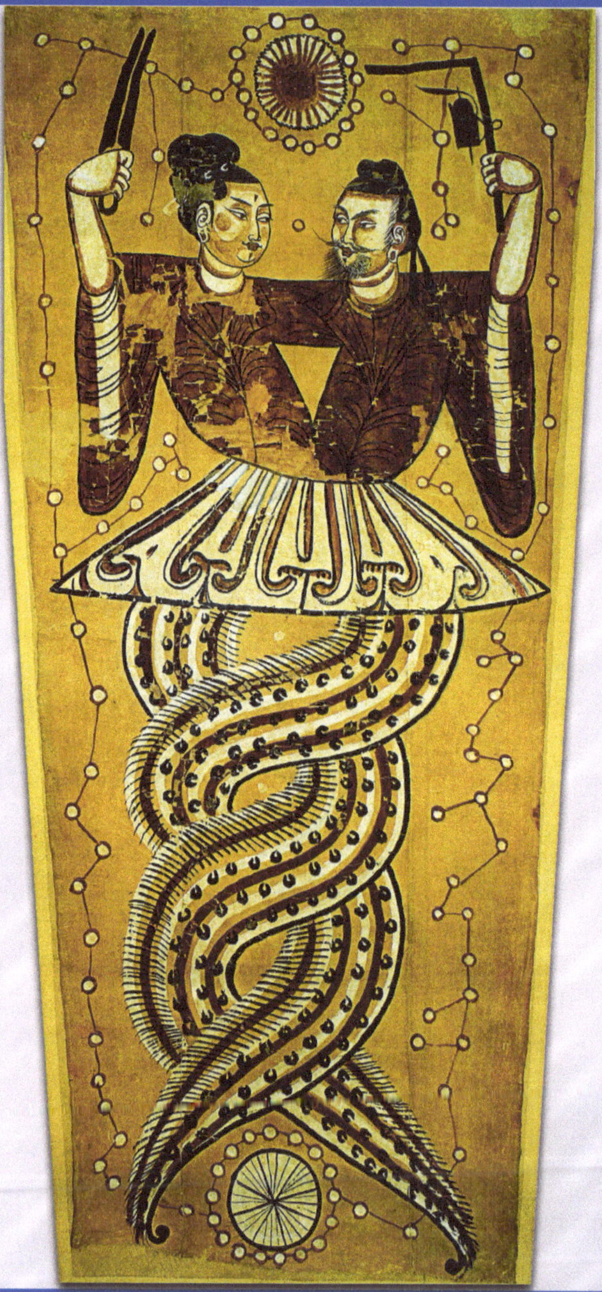

Fu Hsi, Fu Xi, also known as Paoxi. There are a lot of different and contradictory stories about Fu Xi, we are talking about many thousands of years of history so, things change over time. First, he is said to be a creator god who invented hunting, fishing, domestication, and cooking. He also invented the *bagua,* eight three line sets of continuous and broken lines. The continuous lines are called yang, the broken lines, yin. Yang is male the yin, female. Yin and yang are present in everything, bringing them into balance is the big task. The I Ching, the Book of Changes, became the means by which to divine using the yin and yang lines, doing away with the bone oracles previously used for divination. Confucius, many years later, added to the I Ching and it is sometimes, incorrectly, attributed to Him. Fu Xi is present in two of the four flood stories along with his sister Nugua or Nüwa who appears in one of the others alone. Although the floods are caused by the thunder god and make problems for the people involved, they are not sent as heavenly retribution, unlike the flood stories in many other countries. There are also six creation stories. In one the creator god Phugu, after creating the sky and the earth, died, his body turned into all the things in the world; animals, plants, rivers, etc. and a powerful goddess named Huaxu, she became pregnant after stepping in a footprint left by Legong, the thunder god, and gave birth to the twin brother and sister, Fu Xi and Nüwa, said to have human faces and snake bodies. Huaxu carried Fu Xi in her womb for twelve years and delivered Nüwa three months after Fu Xi. Nüwa is also known as the creator goddess who, after the flood, repopulated the earth with humans made from clay, sometimes alone and sometimes with the help of her brother, She was the goddess of matchmakers. She also fixed the pillars holding up heaven. Elsewhere, when the earth first began. Fu Xi and Nüwa are the original humans who decide to become husband and wife in order to populate the earth, but first, they seek guidance from above.* Once their union had been sanctioned by heaven, they still felt some shame so, before becoming intimate, they covered their faces with a woven grass screen. It is said that still today, on their wedding night, couples hold a fan to symbolize what happened long ago.

Fu was also one of the Sanxing "Three Stars," Fu, Lu, and Shou, the gods linked to Jupiter, Ursa Major, and Canopus. Fu presided over Jupiter as the embodiment of **Fortune**, Lu over Ursa Major, **Prosperity**, Shou over Canopus, **Longevity**. Three attributes that represent a good life. Fu can be written in one hundred different ways which allows for a lot of interpretations, fun wordplay and confusion. Fu Xi lived for 197 years.

*Fu Xi and Nüwa's prayer:
Oh Heaven, if Thou wouldst send us forth as man and wife,
then make all the misty vapor gather.
If not, then make all the misty vapor disperse.
The misty vapor gathered, obviously.

Cool Fact: The symbol for Bats has the same symbolic meaning as the ideograph "fortune." Sending someone a picture of bats in flight can be a way of wishing that good fortune comes their way.

What other Gods' names start with F?

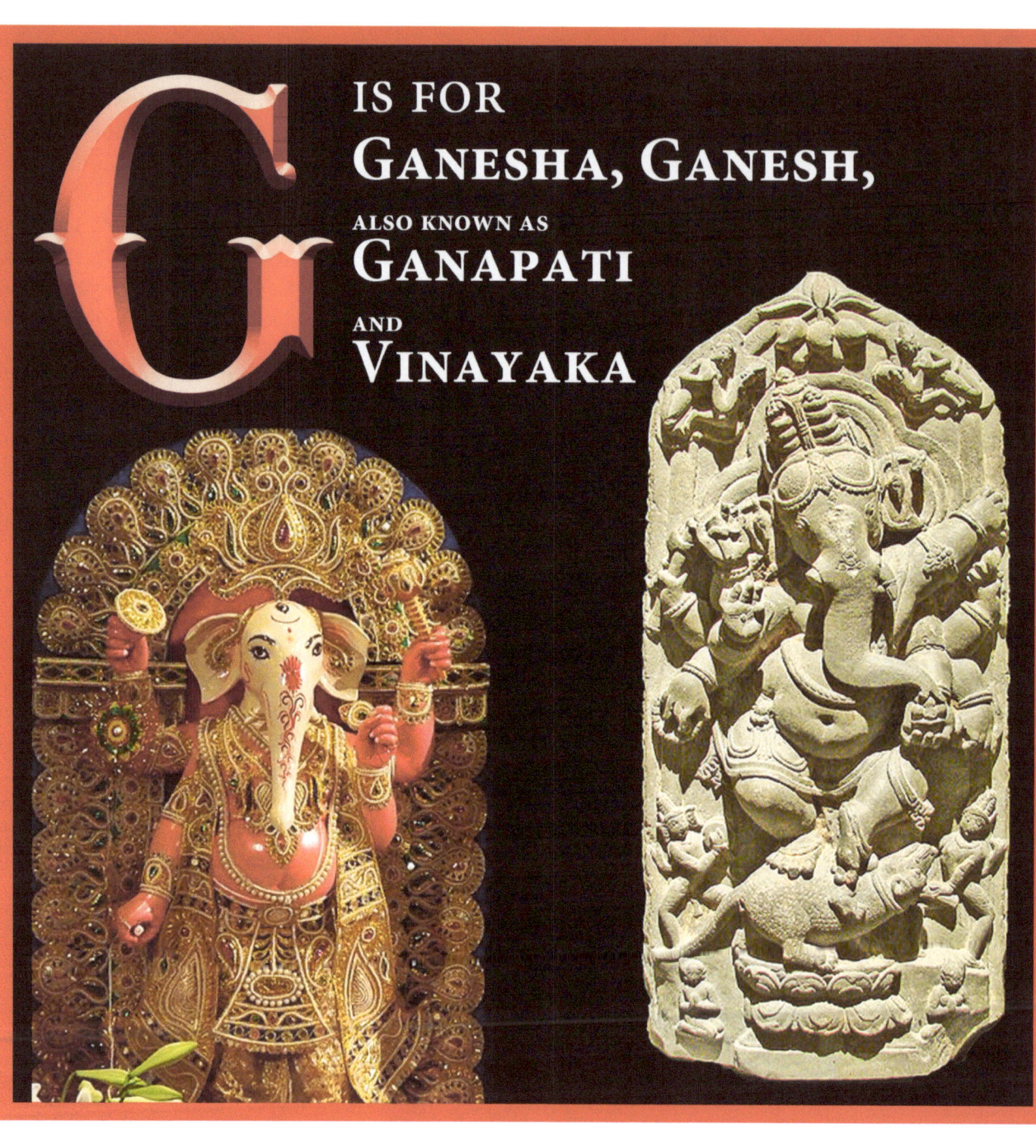

G is for Ganesha, Ganesh,
also known as Ganapati and Vinayaka

G **Ganesha,** is the god of wisdom, intellect, and good fortune. Devotees invoke the name of Ganesha when beginning an activity thereby opening the door to material success and spiritual growth. He is the remover of obstacles and patron of the arts and sciences. In one version of the story, Ganesha is the son of Parvati, the Goddess of fertility, love, beauty, harmony, marriage, children, and devotion, and the god Shiva, god of destruction, destroyer of evil who also creates, protects, and transforms the universe. In another, he was made from clay by Parvati, but in both, he was to guard the door while Parvati bathed. In both, Shiva came along and Ganesha wouldn't allow him to open the door. Shiva, in anger, cuts off Ganesha's head. Parvati orders Shiva to restore the boy's life and his head. Shiva tells his servants to find a head that is pointed north and bring it to him; they bring an elephant's head. In another version Shiva considered Ganesha too alluring so gave him the elephant head and a potbelly. Shiva and Parvati raised Ganesha and his brother Kartikeya, god of war, together although it is said that Shiva spent much of his time on a mountain top meditating. Ganesha may have been celibate or he may have had two or three wives who might have simply been feminine emanations of certain powers named for goddesses. Alternatively. Ganesha was said to be the brother of these goddesses. In Bengal during the Durga Puja ceremony a banana tree is transformed into a goddess who marries Ganesha, or, the banana tree represents Durga Puja who is considered the mother of Ganesha. These stories date back thousands of years. The *Mahabharata,* one of the longest literary works ever produced, was written by several authors over a long period of time, parts of it may be over 2,500yrs. old, but it was supposedly dictated to Ganesha by the sage Vyasa. Since Hinduism is a living religion, these events in the Hindu calendar continue to be celebrated and reenacted throughout India, Nepal, Sri Lanka, Thailand, Bali, Bangladesh, and wherever Indian populations are found. There are populations in Fiji, in Trinidad and Tobago, you will even see Ganesha celebrations in the streets of New York City. Jains and Buddhists are devotees of Ganesha. He is popular in Japan, where he is known as Kangiten, considered to be a Japanese Buddhist form of a Hindu god. The cities of Harappa and Mohenjo-Daro uncovered in the 1920s, were built around 2500BCE and were abandoned around 1900BCE, about the time of the arrival of the Aryans. It was the fusion of the Aryan culture with that of the Harappan civilization that eventually gave rise to Hinduism. The Ganesha Purana is one of four Puranas dedicated to Ganesha, it contains many stories and religious elements relating to him. All of his accoutrements, his potbelly, his arms, from two to sixteen, why he carries the things he has, and a whole lot more is explained therein.

Cool Fact: A Vahana is a being, either an animal or a mythical entity used as a mount or vehicle by Hindu deities. When Ganesha was still a child he trapped a giant mouse that was terrorizing his friends. The mouse was actually a celestial musician who had been transformed into a mouse by a rishi (sage) he had annoyed. Feeling sorry for his actions, the sage told the mouse that one day the gods would bow down before him. Becoming the vahana of Ganesha fulfilled the prophecy.

What other gods' names start with G?

H IS FOR HERMES

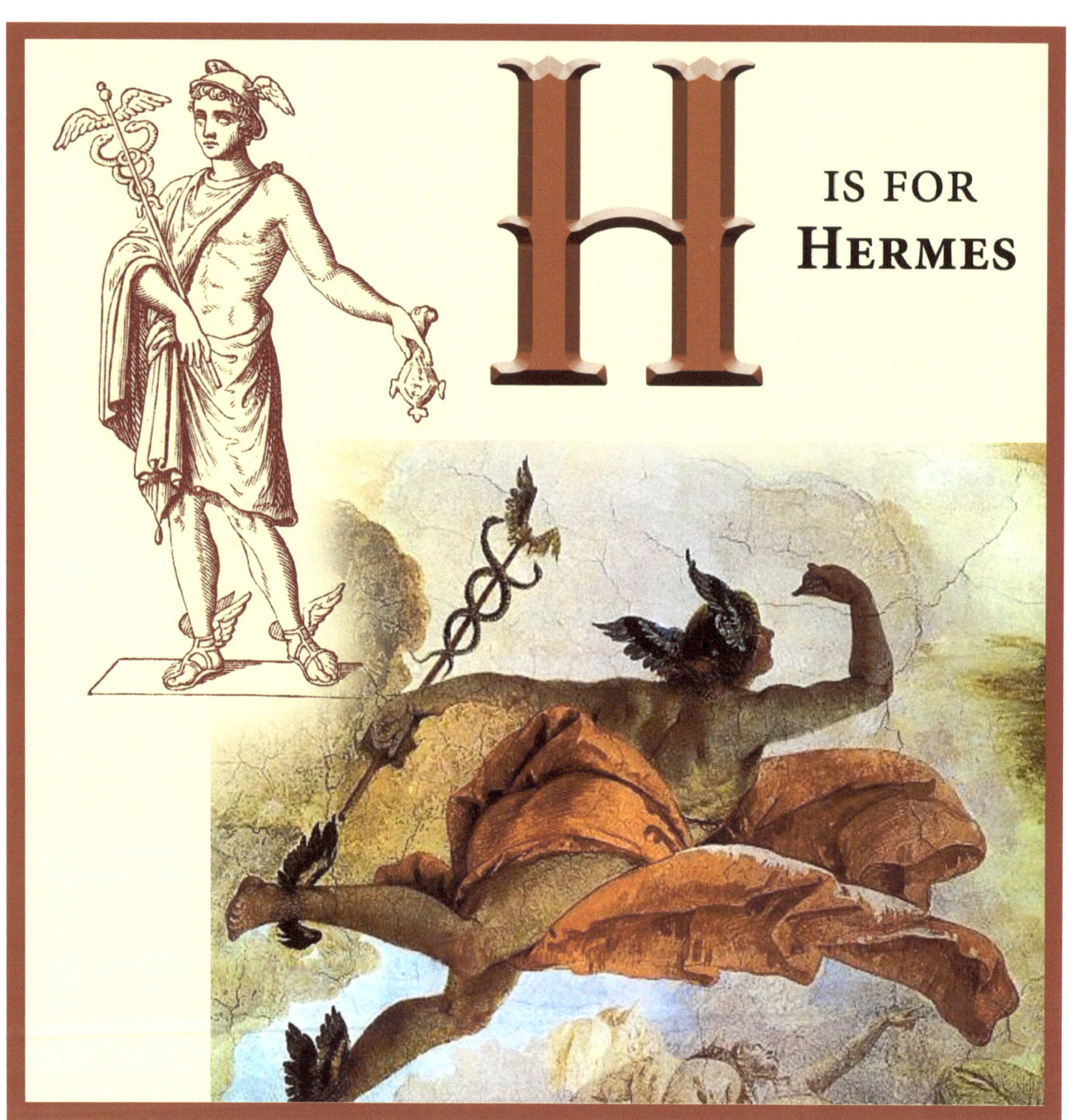

Hermes, god of trade, wealth, luck, fertility, animal husbandry, sleep, language, thieves and travel, credited with inventing fire, the alphabet, dice, (gamblers worship him for the luck and wealth aspects) musical instruments, particularly the lyre, patron of shepherds since he invented the pan pipes. Orators and interpreters worshiped him as patron of languages and rhetoric; the study and interpretation of texts is known as hermeneutics. His name probably derives from, *herma* Greek for a heap of stones such as were used to mark boundaries and landmarks. Stone pillars, (hermae) often with a phallus symbol, along roadsides, acted as guides and offered good fortune to travelers. They also served to remind that he was the messenger between the gods and humanity and that he guided the dead into the next life. As the protector of youths, he was often associated with gymnasia; a healthy body was considered as important as a good education, young men from the upper classes would spend a good part of every day exercising in the gymnasiums or sports centers outside Athens. The *hermaia* festival for young boys was held annually in Athens, in Crete at a sanctuary dedicated to him, young men about to become full citizens, engaged in a two-month-long rite of cultivating homosexual relationships with older men. This and another Cretan festival where slaves were permitted to temporarily take the place of their masters, celebrated Hermes' association with crossing boundaries. In art Hermes is shown holding the caduceus staff entwined with two snakes, signifying his role as herald, winged sandals as messenger, sometimes a winged cap, sometimes a lyre, (he made from a tortoiseshell) Sometimes a ram, sometimes an infant Hercules or Achilles, indicating his association with youths. Other icons might be shown linking him to the wide variety of activities to which he was patron. Above all, as if that wasn't enough, he was herald and messenger to the gods of Olympus. He had the typical powers of an Olympian; superhuman strength, durability, stamina, agility, and reflexes. He could run and fly faster than any other Olympian god or goddess. He was persuasive and eloquent which led to his association with diplomacy that he tainted somewhat by his fondness for mischief, trickery, shiftiness, and dishonesty.

The Romans, lacking the basics of civilization, took the Greek pantheon of gods, together with everything else they could, renaming them to create their own mythological history. Hermes became Mercury, retaining the role of messenger and all of Hermes' other positions. The word merchant is derived from Mercury in his role as god of trade. Mercury orbits the sun faster than all the other planets.

Cool Fact: A misunderstanding of mythology and iconography seems to have led to the caduceus of Hermes being adopted as the symbol of medicine by the US Army Medical Corps., and later for the medical profession. It is the single snake entwined staff of Aesculapius, Asclepius, the god of healing, that's the internationally recognized symbol of medicine. Snakes were sacred beings of wisdom, healing, and resurrection. A species of non-venomous snake, one of the largest snakes in Europe, the Aesculapian snake, *(Zamenis longissimus)* is named for the god.
What other gods' names start with H?

I

IS FOR
INTI

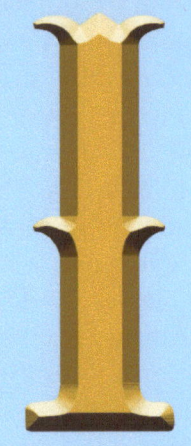

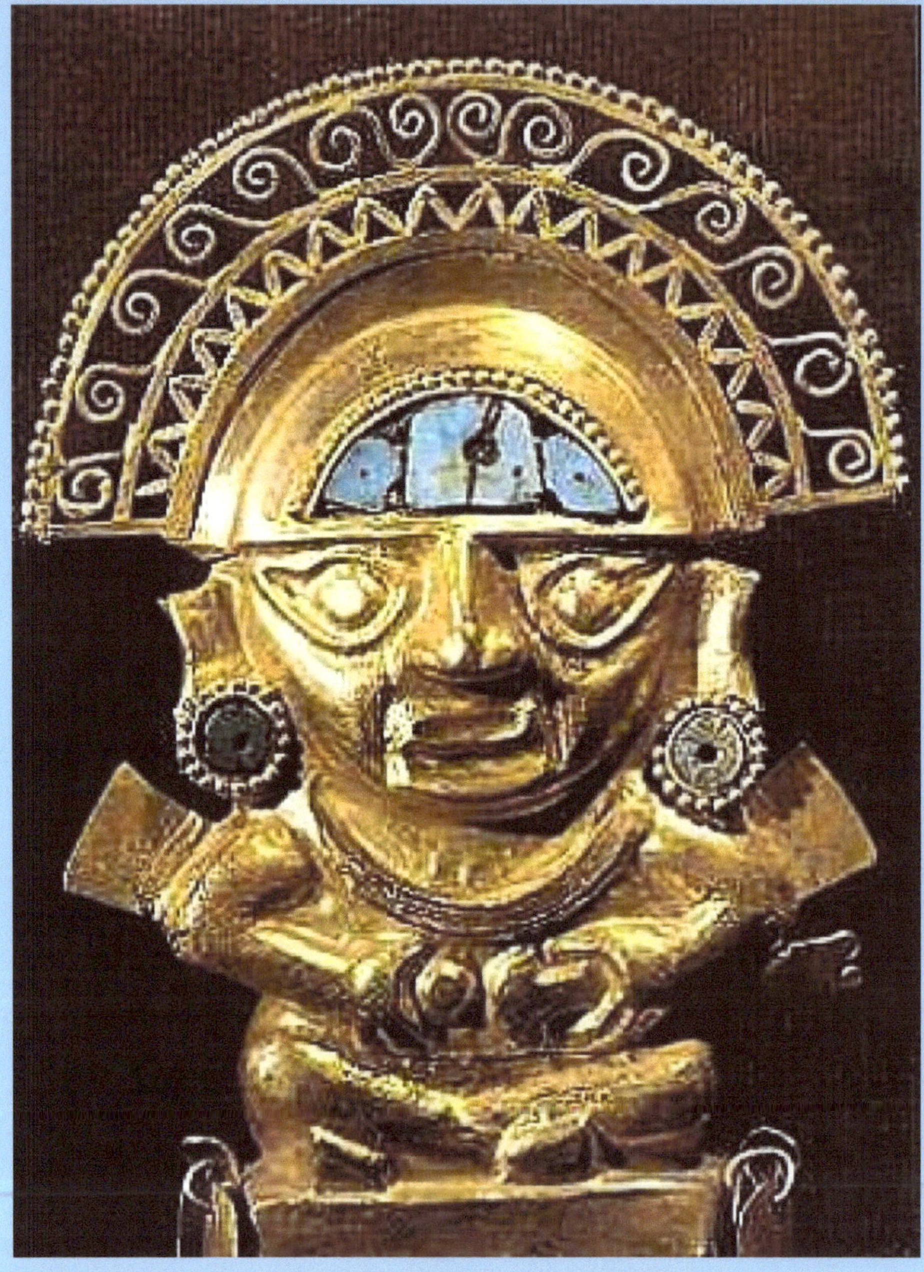

Inti the ancient Inca sun god was worshiped as the patron deity of the Inca Empire but, since the Inca gave different identities to the stages of the sun he could more appropriately be considered a cluster of solar aspects. Apu Inti, supreme and father Inti, Churi Inti, son of Inti was "Daylight, associated with the summer solstice, and Inti Wawqi, "Sun brother" the three diurnal stages of the sun. The Inti Raymi'rata annual winter solstice sun festival held on June 24th in Cusco, the ancient capital of the Inca was attended by everybody who was anybody, dressed up in their finest with their best weapons and instruments. It was a nine-day festival during which massive amounts of food and drink were consumed however, it began with three days of fasting when no fires were lit and sexual intercourse was forbidden. There were human sacrifices on the first day. It has become a big tourist attraction. The Inca had no written language, paintings on vases, and depictions in other media gave visual narratives, dates and amounts were recorded on *quipus,* knotted strings, it is possible that they also recorded events and more but the Spanish destroyed most *quipu* before they could be deciphered. It is known that Manco Cápac first governor and founder of the Inca civilization, and his tribe managed to get a foothold in a part of the Cusco valley in the early 13th century. The creation myth says that Inti and Mama Killa, the Moon Goddess, his older sister, were also man and wife. She bore him two sons. One of the sons was Manco who was also worshiped as a Fire and Sun God, he and his siblings were sent down to earth by Inti bearing a divine golden staff, or wedge in some versions, with the instructions that wherever the wedge sank into the ground, that was the place to build a temple to the Sun. Cusco was the place. From there the Inca empire spread to include at its height, Peru, West and South Central Bolivia, SW Ecuador, and a large part of Chile. "*Inka*" means "ruler" or "lord" in Quechua, the language of the Inca, and referred only to the ruling family and classes, the vast population of the Inca empire was not *Inka*. The Spanish adopted the term, changed it to Inca, and applied it to all the subjects of the Inca empire. Those who followed the Inca moral code, "do not steal, do not lie, do not be lazy", "went to live in the Sun's warmth," those that did not, "Spent their eternal days in the cold earth."

The predominance of sun worship around the world begs the question, is there an innate understanding of the role the sun plays in our lives, or has the idea of the sun as a god simply been handed down through the millennia? Oral traditions have extraordinary staying power. It's easy to see how a story told in Sumeria makes its way up through The Middle East, we have written records, but across the world to another continent and a people who have no alphabet and no means of transmission other than human feet and the spoken word? The Sun of May appears on the flags of Argentina and Uruguay, it is also the national emblem of those countries. Early designs of the flag of Peru featured the Inti sun image. The sun is also on the coat of arms of Bolivia, Argentina, and Ecuador. Even the flag of Hispanicity, sometimes used to represent Hispanic people, has the Inti sun rising behind three crosses.

Cool Fact: There are 100-400 billion stars similar to our sun in the Milky Way alone, that being just one galaxy of perhaps trillions in the universe that we can see. The American astronomer Carl Sagan likened our planet to, "a mote of dust suspended in a sunbeam."
What other gods' names start with I?

J IS FOR JIMMU-TENNŌ

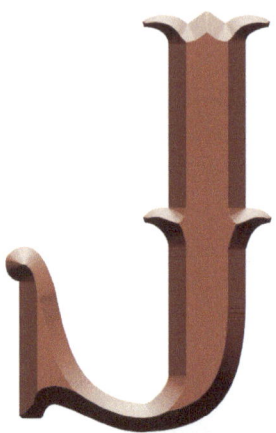

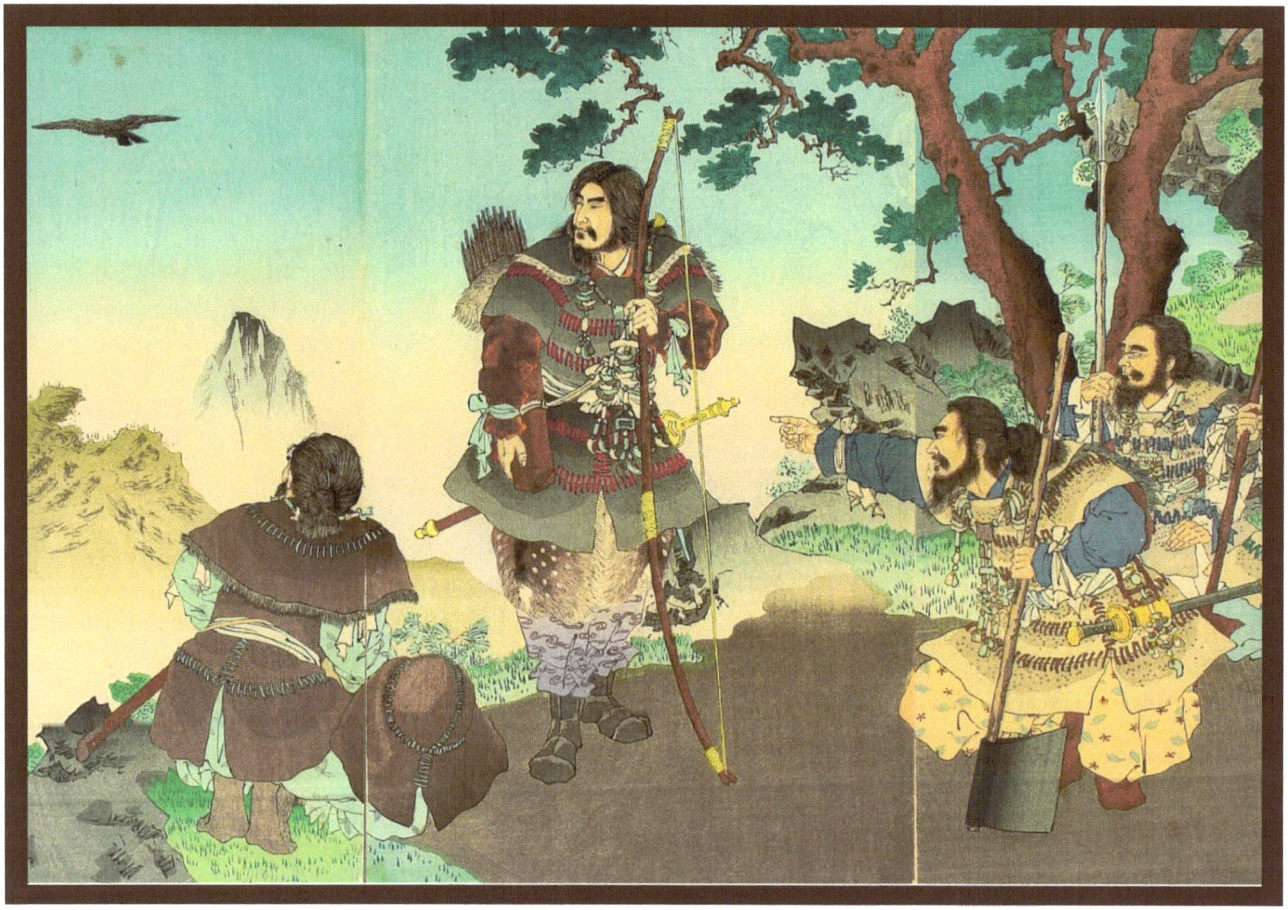

Jimmu-tennō (Jimmu means "divine might" or "divine warrior emperor," tennō, "heavenly sovereign," whose reign lasted from 660-585BCE was believed to be the great, great, great grandson of the divine sun goddess Amaterasu. Amaterasu was born from the eye of the primal Creator god Izanagi. Known as "the august person who makes the heaven shine," she was assigned to rule the heavens, one of her brothers Tsuki-Yomi, ruled the night as the moon god. Another, Susano was the god of storms and the forces of disorder. A whole lot goes down between the siblings and the other gods and goddesses, some nasty and some naughty before we get to Jimmu-tennō.

In a move to expand their territory, Jimmu and his brother Itsuse no Mikoto, who lived at the southern tip of the island of Kyūshū led their clan into battle, Itsuse was killed. Jimmu realizing that they had been defeated because they had battled east, towards the sun, decided to battle westward, with the guidance of a three legged crow he was successful and ascended to the throne. As the "heavenly sovereign," he was the first legendary Emperor of Japan. When surveying the Seto inland sea, now part of his domain, he remarked how it resembled the "heart" shape made by mating dragonflies. When a mosquito tried to steal his royal blood, a dragonfly killed the mosquito. This is why Japan or Nippon in Japanese, became known as the dragonfly islands.

So much for the legend: there were no emperors at the time Jimmu is said to have lived and unless you believe in goddesses, he couldn't have been born. Historians date the imperial line to the 5th or 6th century CE. It was the Yamamoto emperors who selected Amaterasu as their ancestress in a line directly from Jimmu-tennō, designating him as the first of Japan's emperors, meant that all of those that followed could claim descent from Amaterasu the sun goddess. Thus, the flag of Japan with its "rising sun," Nippon, the correct name for Japan, means "rising sun," and stands for Amaterasu. The stories linking the gods and goddesses to the emperor, together with Buddhism and Confucianism, from China, blended in, became known as Shinto ("the way of the gods") the state religion of Japan.

Tales of warrior emperors and militarism in general gave rise to a warrior class, the samurai. Known for their fighting skills and knightly values, most samurai were more like security guards, protecting aristocrats and their property. Many had little to do and spent their time sitting around getting drunk and gambling.

Legends die hard, so we see a mausoleum at the site where Jimmu is believed to be buried, (having died at 127 yrs. of age) and in 1890 a Shinto shrine dedicated to him was built within walking distance of the mausoleum. There are numerous Emperor Jimmu Sacred Historical Sites. Every spring a festival, affectionately named "Jimmusai" is held. It is possible that all the myths reflect some actual events in the distant past but, facts are dull compared to fantasy.

Cool Fact: After the Second World War, with the American forces occupying Japan, Emperor Hirohito announced, to the consternation of many of his subjects, that, contrary to popular belief, he was not divine. State Shintoism ended and Japan became a parliamentary democracy with the emperor, no longer a god, as head of state.

What other gods' names start with J?

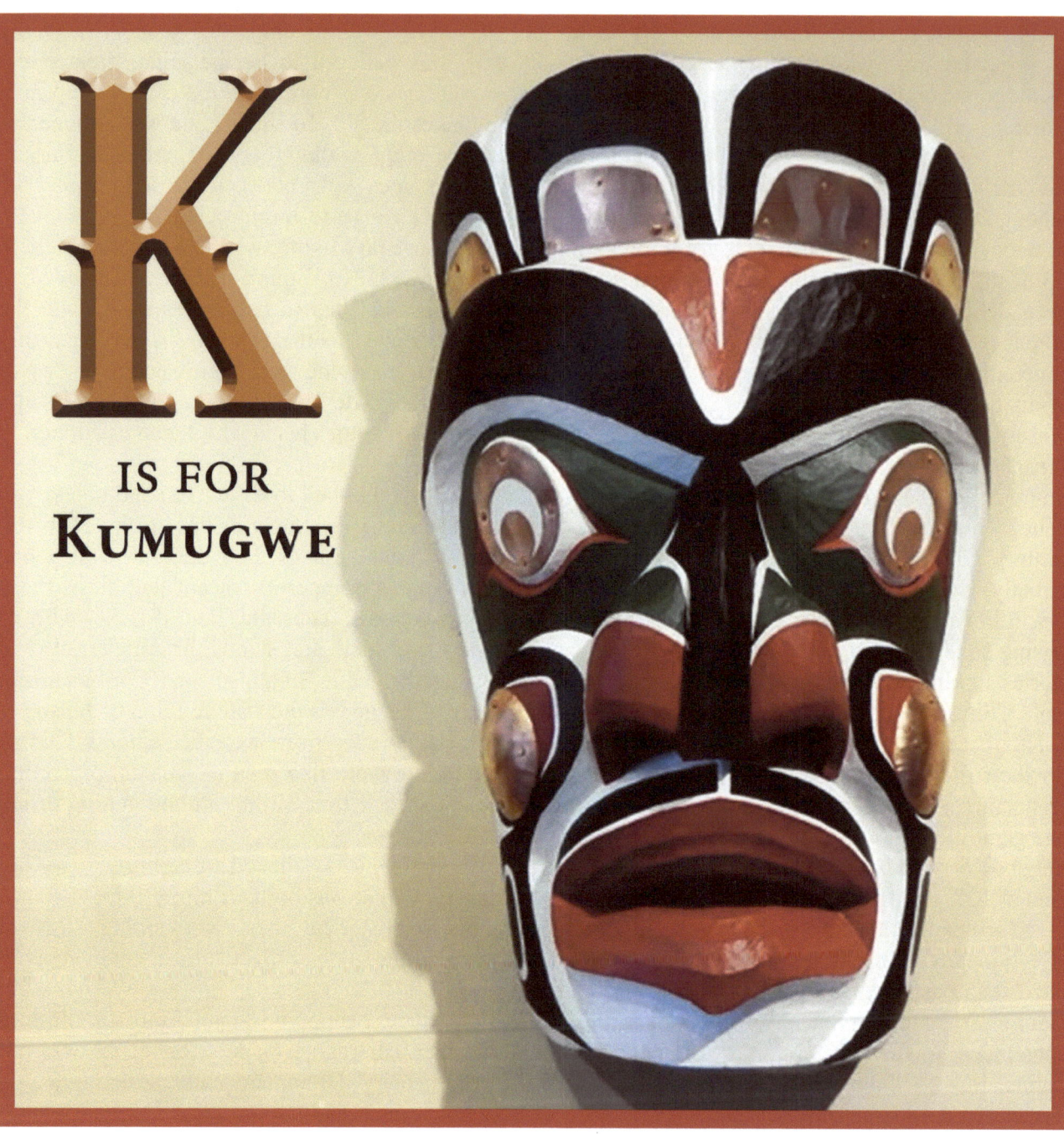

K

IS FOR KUMUGWE

Kumugwe, is the undersea world god of the Kwakwaka'wakw people of British Columbia and northern Vancouver island in western Canada. His kingdom is made of copper and he is known as the "Copper Maker," his wife Tlakwakilayokwa's name means "Born to be Copper Makers woman." His name means "wealthy one" and his house under the sea is filled with riches, its posts and beams are living sea lions. Loons, seals, sea lions, octopus, and sculpin (a ray-finned bottom-dwelling fish of ocean and freshwater zones,) are his most important totemic animals. His world is guarded by octopus. He is responsible for the ebb and flow of the tides and for any riches that are found on the beaches (washed out of his house, perhaps}, he is responsible for the vagaries of the sea weather and all that it claims, both material and human lives. He can see into the future, and heal the sick and injured. If he favors any that venture into his abode, he will bestow powers upon them, teach them the ways of the sea, and shower them with gifts, blankets, copper, songs, masks, and regalia, (he's got all that stuff in his house, remember?) Kumugwe masks often have rounded fish eyes, gills around the mouth, fins around his head, and the suction cups of octopus. Such items are called Tlugwe 'supernatural treasure,' they are stored and hidden in Kwakwaka'wakw clan houses to be used only by those initiates selected to represent the ancients in ceremonies meant to connect the world of the living with the world of the spirits.

Indigenous people have occupied the Pacific Northwest Coast for many thousands of years crossing from Siberia by the land bridge that once existed or by sailing across. Spreading down the coast, the region from British Columbia, Washington state, Alaska, Oregon, and Northern California once had the highest population of Indigenous people in the Americas. Fishing, particularly of salmon and whaling, became the way of life, moving with the seasons from the coast into the lush forests of cedar and conifers, used for housing and for their sea-going boats. As elsewhere, infectious diseases brought by the European explorers and traders devastated their populations. Today, there are around 5,500 Kwakwaka'wakw in 17 separate tribes on Vancouver Island and the mainland. Still dependent on Kumugwe for the bounty of the sea.

Cool Fact: Starfish once were women transformed by Mink, the trickster deity, as punishment for their having defied him. Starfish are part of Kumugwe's wealth and traditional carvings of him are often adorned with starfish.

What other gods' names start with K?

L

IS FOR
Lugh

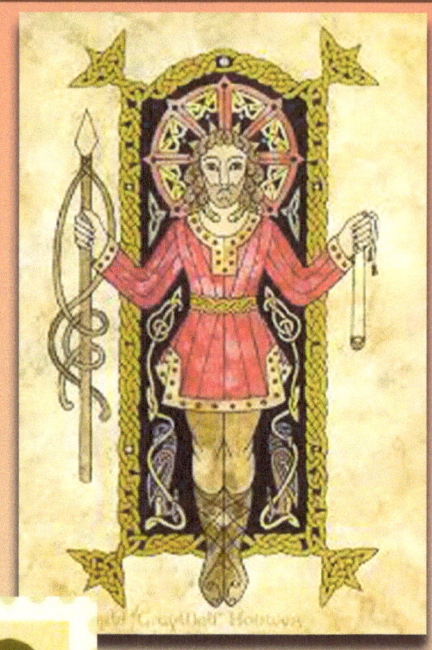

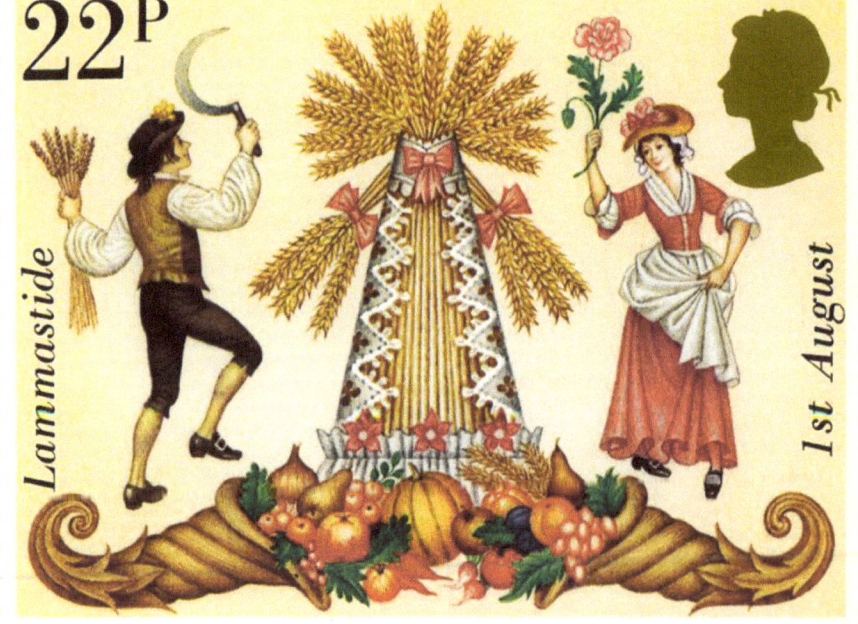

Lammastide — 1st August — 22P

L **Lugh**, pronounced loo, was the Celtic god of sunshine and light. He was the patron of scholars, craftsmen, warriors, and magicians for this he was known as Lugh Samildánach (the Many Skilled) and Lugh Lámhafada (Lugh of the Long Arm) either for his spear that guaranteed victory, for the sword he forged that cut through anything, or for the rays of sunlight he emitted. The Celts, usually pronounced, Kelts, of Ireland trace back to semi-nomadic people of Indo-European origin who moved into northern Europe then spread to western Europe, some of them crossing into the British Isles around 400BC then to Ireland around 350BC. The Celts were feared by Roman legionnaires as semi-naked wild men, they had burned Rome in 390BC and invaded Greece in 272BC. Most of what we have in the way of Irish history was written hundreds of years after the events and myths are generously woven into the story. The Tuatha "the people of the goddess Danu," the Firblogs and the Formorians fought among themselves, as families will, Nuadu (Nudd) the supreme god of the Irish Celtic pantheon and ruler of the Tuatha lost his throne, then regained it after receiving a magic silver arm but, he retired and gave the throne up to Lugh, "the Shining God" of the Celts who was related by blood to the Tuatha and the Formorians. I know, it's complicated.

Lúnasa is the month of August in modern Gaelic, the Lugnasadh Festival is celebrated on August 1st. The ancient Celts probably held it on the full moon closest to that date, halfway between the summer solstice and the autumn equinox, it marks the beginning of harvest time. In the British Isles Lammas is celebrated at this time, throughout the northern climate zone, harvest time is a time for celebration and a time to prepare for the coming winter months. Fairs and athletic contests are held and the first fruits of the harvest are offered to the gods. The Lugnasadh "Commemoration of Lugh" is also a celebration of Lugh's wedding or a funeral rite for Tailtin, Lugh's foster mother, who cleared the land for crops then died from exhaustion afterward, or all of the above. It is also seen as celebrating the triumph over those spirits of the Otherworld who would try to keep the harvest from the people and for themselves. There are countless tales of Lugh's adventures and exploits, he was finally killed by a son of Dagda, one of the Tuatha gods who could control life and death, the weather and crops, time, and the seasons. At his death, Lugh had ruled for forty years. But wait, do gods die? There may be more tales ahead.

Cool Fact: After their defeat, the Tuatha retreated to underground mounds called *sidh*. They show up in Irish legends as the "little people" the Leprechauns. Although, once again, that name is said to derive from Lugh's role as the craftsman Lugh Chromain ("little stooping Lugh") being anglicized into "leprechaun."

What other gods' names start with L?

M
IS FOR
Marduk

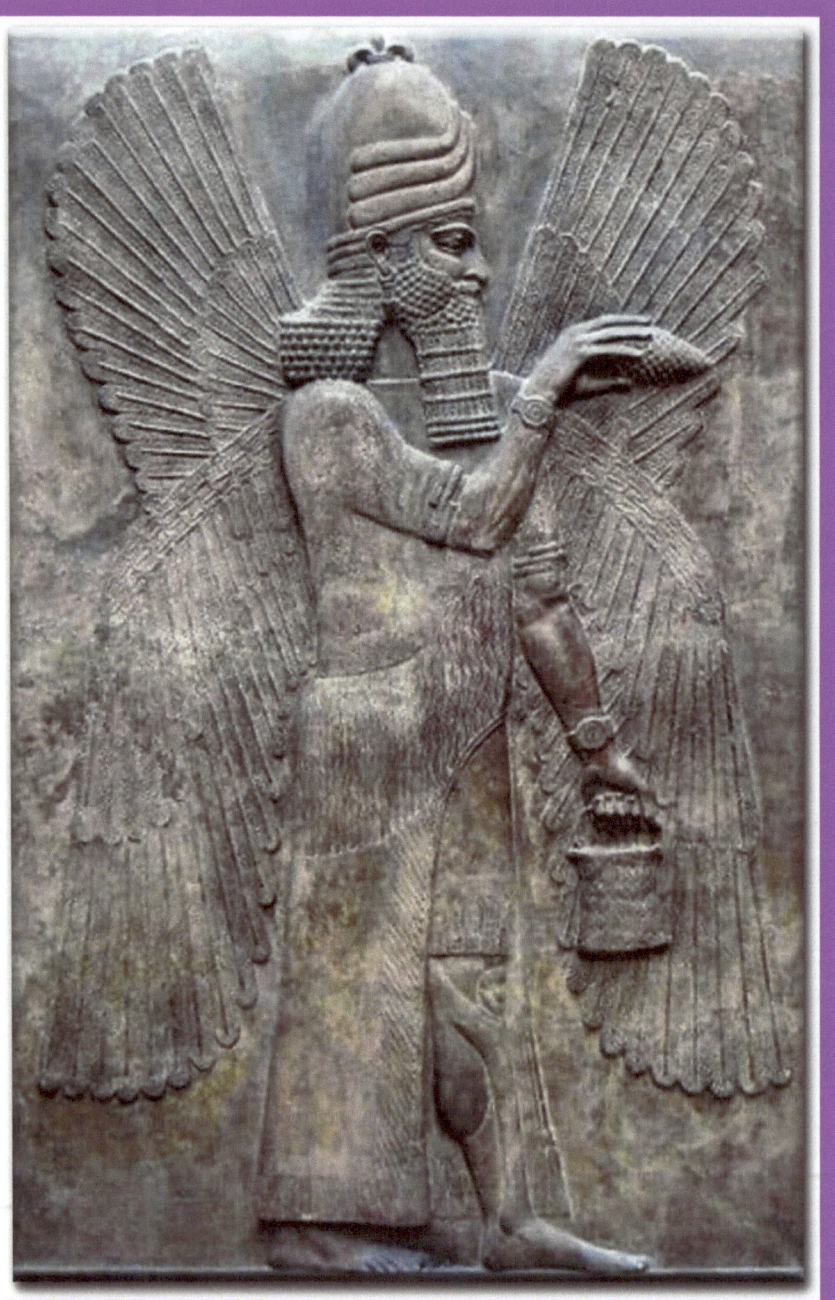

Marduk, Bel, Baal. When Herodotus wrote in his "The Histories" of the great seated gold figure on a golden throne, of the golden altar upon which tons of frankincense were placed each year on the festival of Bel, he was actually referring to Marduk, as Bel and Baal mean "Lord" the titles of Babylon's central deity. The Babylonian Empire arose around 1900BCE to become the greatest in Mesopotamia. Translated as "gate of the gods," "Babylon" was believed by the people to be the place where the gods came down to earth. The *Enuma Elish,* Mesopotamia's creation myth reads like a horror story as the fight of the warring gods for supremacy unfolds. At first, there were just two, Apsu, representing freshwater, and the goddess Tiamat, saltwater. When these two joined they produced Lahmu and Lahamu and then Anu and Ea. Noisy kids that they were, their parents couldn't sleep so Apsu decided to destroy them all. When son Ea found out his plan, he put Apsu asleep, killed him, and took his place as god of the waters. Tiamat, naturally upset, created a small army of monsters, turned herself into a fearsome dragon with the aim of completing the job Apsu had planned. Marduk, the son of Ea and his wife, being the sun god and the "highest among the gods", offered to fight his grandmother on behalf of the rest of the gods so long as he could be their ruler. He battled the monsters and destroyed them, then he faced off with Grandma dragon. In the words of the *Enuma Elish;*
"The Lord trampled the lower part of Tiamat,
   with his unsparing mace smashed her skull,
      severed the arteries of her blood"
Slicing her in half he used one part to create the sky and with the other, the earth. The Tigris and Euphrates rivers he created from her eyes. Her breasts he transformed into the mountains from where freshwater flows. With that out of the way, he organized the universe, named the months of the year, created the stars and the moon, devised laws, and set up a city he called Babylon as his home. Oh yes! Then he created man by mixing the blood of Tiamat's husband with dust. From then on, man would do the work and the gods could relax but, before that, they built a Ziggurat as a temple where Marduk could be worshiped as King of the gods.

The Mesopotamians picked up a lot of their mythology from the Sumerians but that didn't stop Marduk from destroying Sumer's sky god, An or Anu, by flaying him alive, cutting off his head, and tearing his heart out. He killed off An's son Enlil too while he was about it. Being passed on over thousands of years, it is little wonder that the many versions contradict one another as different cultures adopted them. The symbolic meaning of those stories was likely not even known by the priests charged with relating them.

Cool Fact: The gold statue of Marduk was removed from Babylon by invaders several times, causing great disruption. Each time the city was sacked it was taken, then brought back again. The son of one of those invading kings voluntarily brought the statue back and built a new temple to honor Marduk. Later the city streets were widened so that the statue could be paraded with more pomp during festivals. After such celebrations, it was taken to a small house outside the city walls where he could have a different view and enjoy the fresh air.   **What other god's names start with M?**

N IS FOR **NEPTUNE**

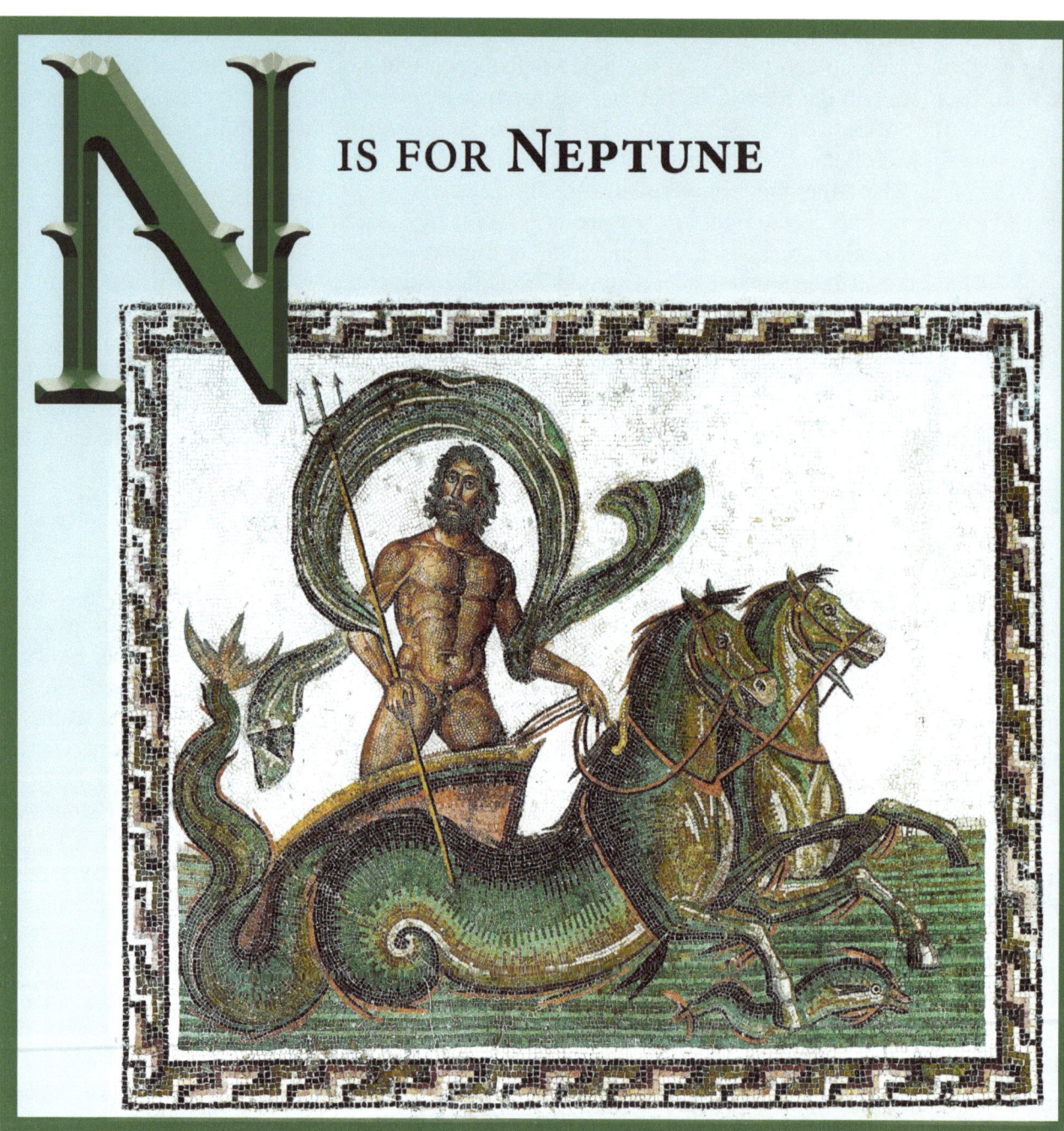

Neptune was the Roman god of freshwater and the sea, his brothers were Jupiter and Pluto. Since it was Jupiter who overthrew their father, Saturn, he got to rule the Earth and sky, Pluto got the Underworld, Neptune got water. Before the Romans were so heavily influenced by all things Greek, Neptune is believed to have been a god of freshwater springs, lakes, and rivers, only becoming associated with the sea when he took on the Greek god Poseidon's attributes. Once that happened, like Poseidon, he was the god of horses and the patron of horse racing, (he got to be the lord of horses by working with the goddess Minerva on inventing the chariot.) Minerva, like Neptune, was probably an Etruscan deity originally, as a Roman goddess she was the equivalent of Athena, Greek goddess of wisdom, handicrafts, warfare, and a whole lot more. Neptune's abode became the sea, his symbols, the horse, the trident, and the dolphin. In his new home, Neptune fell for Salicia, goddess of the wide-open sea, she was overwhelmed by such attention and slid off to hide in the Atlantic Ocean. Neptune was devastated, knowing how much she liked dolphins, he sent one of his to find her and persuade her to come back. Dolphin suggested that her steadiness would balance his turbulence and together there would be harmony at sea. She was persuaded and agreed to marry Neptune. He was so overjoyed he awarded the dolphin his very own constellation, Delphinius, (this story is taken directly from that of Poseidon and Amphitrite.) Various other cultures recognize the constellation, which is close to the celestial equator, giving it their own names.

Salicia was joined by Venilia, also associated with the winds and the sea, together they represent the fundamental powers of Neptune, Salicia being the force of gushing water while Venilia was the still or slow flowing aspect of water. It is questioned whether they were, in fact, just the two faces of water embodied in one person. Either way, they balanced Neptune's ill-tempered and violent nature, (perhaps caused by the trauma of having been eaten by his father in infancy) that was responsible for the ocean's turbulence, and for earthquakes, at that time thought to be caused by storms at sea.

A two-day festival was held in Rome every July 23rd public games were held, two other festivals were celebrated around that time, all being devoted to water in some way. Citizens got out of their houses to picnic and enjoy nature, they built shelters of branches and foliage for shade and perhaps prayed for a little rain to relieve the summer drought.

Statues of Neptune are to be found in various cities around the world, in Berlin, Germany, The Neptunbrunnen, Neptune Fountain, built in 1891 has a statue of Neptune in the middle with four women around him representing the four rivers of Prussia, the Elbe, the Rhine, the Vistula and Oder. Originally located at the Schlossplatz, it was removed, restored, and moved to its present location in 1969 near the Rotes Rathaus, Berlin's town hall.

Cool Fact: Neptune, the eighth planet from the sun, was discovered in 1846, shortly thereafter, its largest moon was observed, it was named for Neptune's son, Triton.

What other gods' names start with N?

O

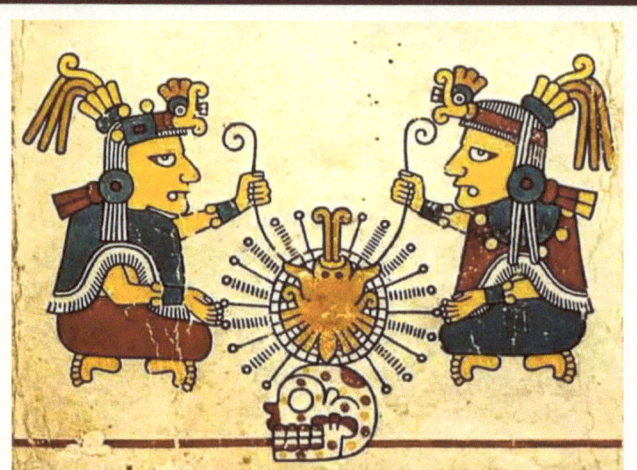

IS FOR

OMETECUHTLI, OMETEŌTL

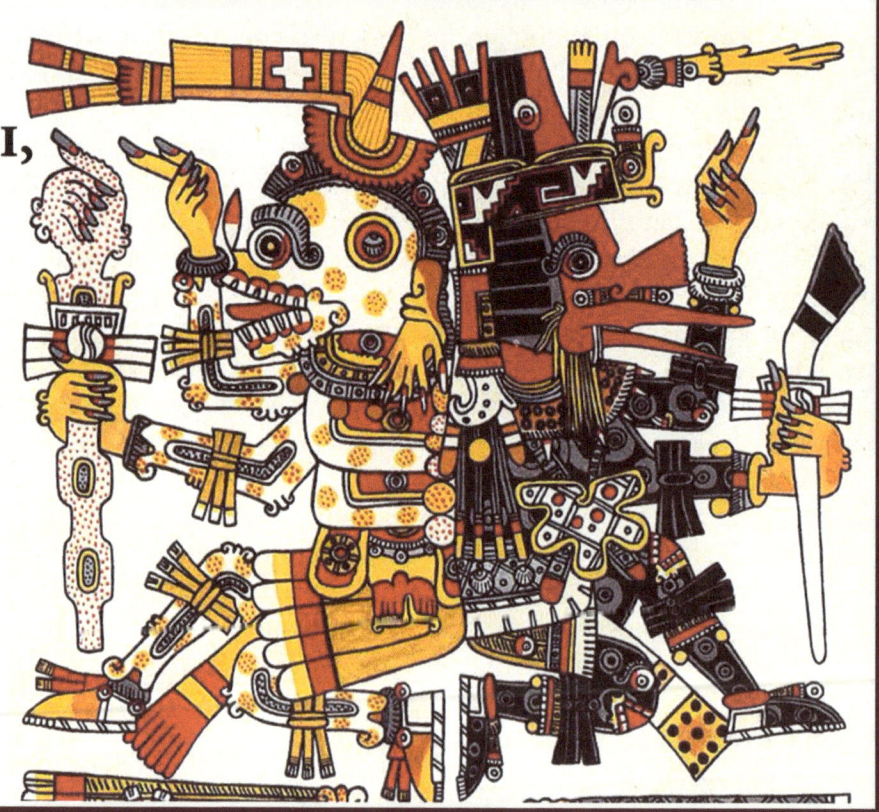

Ometecuhtli, pronounced- o me-te-cuhtli, "the dual lord," the androgynous lord of duality, together with Omecihuatl, they make Two Lord and Two Lady, they live in Omtycan or Omeyocan, the Place Two, the highest Aztec heaven, no. 13. They are the patrons of the first day of the ritual calendar, the original generation, and "the Lord and Lady of our flesh and sustenance." They are represented by symbols of fertility and adorned with ears of corn. Like all religious concepts, ideas, and rituals are derived from older practices. The concept of the dual creative principle predates the Aztec. It may have been a concept too far for the Spanish Fathers, particularly one that more or less amounted to transvestism. Given that so much of the history and culture of the indigenous people was destroyed, both intentionally and unintentionally, by the Spanish, that idea would be high on the list as one that had to go. In one version of their story Ometecuhtli and Omecihuatl have four sons; Red Tezcatlipoca, also known as Xipe, Black Tezcatlipoca, Quetzalcoatl and Huitzilopochtli, who were often depicted as half man and half woman, to whom was entrusted the creation of the other gods, the world, and mankind. That wouldn't leave much for the folks to do, and in fact, Ometecuhtli and Omecihuatl were so remote up there in the highest heaven that the Aztec expected no interaction with him/her, there was no temple and no formal cult activity attached to them while as the supreme creator god, he/she was seen in every aspect of nature. With so little to go on and the difficulty of translating a language about which, little is known, especially as to how it was spoken, and how little text there is available, it is not surprising that some scholars contend that their names were misinterpreted and no such deity even existed. One scholar could read; "ay ōmeteōtl ya téyocōyani," as "two god creator of humanity," another sees it as, "ayometeotl," meaning, "juicy maguey god," worshiped by drunks, presumably.

The Franciscan missionary, Fra. Bernadino Sahagún, 1499-1590, spent 61yrs. preaching and teaching in Mexico, he became the first anthropologist in the New World and preserved much of the traditions and culture he was sent to eliminate. He wrote that Aztec midwives, on cutting the umbilical cord of a newborn, said the following; '*Precious necklace, precious feather, precious green stone, precious bracelet, precious turquoise, thou wert created in the place of duality, the place above the nine heavens. Thy father Ometecuhtli, Omecihuatl, the heavenly woman, formed thee, created thee, (sent thee)...*'

Cool Fact: Dualism usually involves opposites; good versus evil, light and dark, one being the antithesis of the other. With the notion of Yinyang, yin being passive and female, yang being active and male, they are not seen as radically separate but complementary, they permeate each other. Two Lord and Two Lady.

What other gods' names start with O?

P

IS FOR

PAN

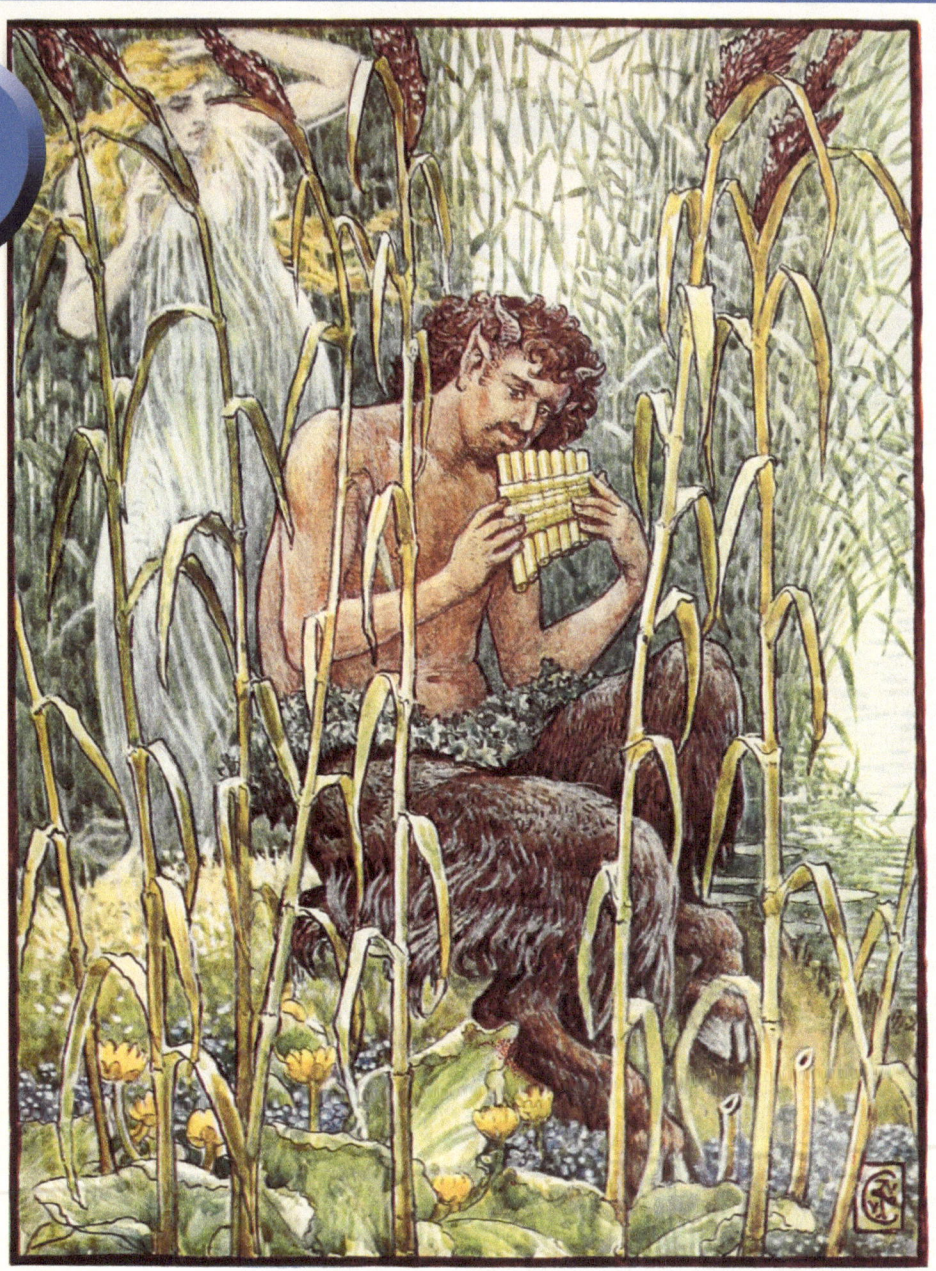

Pan god of the wild, of shepherds and their flocks, keeping company with the nymphs, (usually depicted as beautiful maidens) personifications of nature, subgroups consist of; the Meliae (ash-tree nymphs,) Naiada,(freshwater nymphs) Nereid,(sea nymphs) and Oread(mountain nymphs.) With the hindquarters, legs, and horns of a goat, being affiliated with sex, Pan is also connected to fertility and springtime. A Greek god, Pan is considered to be a carry-over from Proto-Indo-European mythology, his home was Arcadia, a region in the central Peloponnese, celebrated as an unspoiled, harmonious wilderness, Arcadia came to be equated with utopia. A rustic people, the Arcadians were culturally separated from the other Greek people, they worshiped Pan, not in temples or buildings but, in caves or grottos, there is a cave on the north slope of the Acropolis in Athens, Greece, called the cave of Pan. The ruins of a temple to Pan were found in the Peloponnese and there was another in Egypt.

A sculpture found in Pompeii shows Pan teaching his *eromenos,* (an adolescent boy, the passive partner in a homosexual relationship) Daphnis, to play the flute. That flute, known as the Syrinx, which Pan is seldom seen without, is named for the wood-nymph Syrinx of Arcadia. Lecherous Pan, seeing the lovely maiden, pursued her, fleeing to her sisters she asked them to hide her. They turned her into a reed. Unable to identify which reed she was, he cut seven pieces, (some versions say nine) joined them together in decreasing lengths, forming the pan pipes, thus, he could pour his love into playing. Another nymph he loved named Pitys, was turned into a pine tree to avoid him. The nymph Echo so angered Pan that he had her killed, torn to pieces, and scattered all over the world. Now gone, her voice can still be heard in certain locations, repeating the last word of others.

His parentage is murky, he was either the son of Hermes and the nymphs Dryope, Penelope, or Oeneis, or of Zeus and a nymph named Hybris, or of Apollo and Penelope, the wife of Odysseus, or of Hermes and Penelope, or, Penelope gave birth to him after sleeping with all 180 of her suitors (Penelope was actually faithful to Odysseus.) Family values don't figure high in his story.

Unlike some gods, Pan stuck around. In Gloucester, England in the 19th century, an annual parade dedicated to Pan was held. The festival only ended in 1950 when a vicar, frowning on a pagan festival, had Pan's statue buried. Pan appears in a poem by John Keats and in numerous novels and children's books. He is the "Piper at the Gates of Dawn" in *The Wind in the Willows* and is in works as diverse as that of Robert Louis Stevenson, Robert Frost and Tom Robbins, to name but a few. Peter Pan is described as 'a betwix and between' part human part animal, he's both charming and selfish, just like the god Pan.

Cool Fact: Pan's angry shouts created panic (panikon deima) in those he was against. He took credit for the Olympian's victory over the Titans in the war to decide who would rule the universe, saying he had frightened the old gods, the Titans, with his yells. In the battle of Marathon (490BC) he claimed to have panicked the Persians, bringing victory to the Greeks.

What other god's names start with P?

Q IS FOR Quetzalcoatl

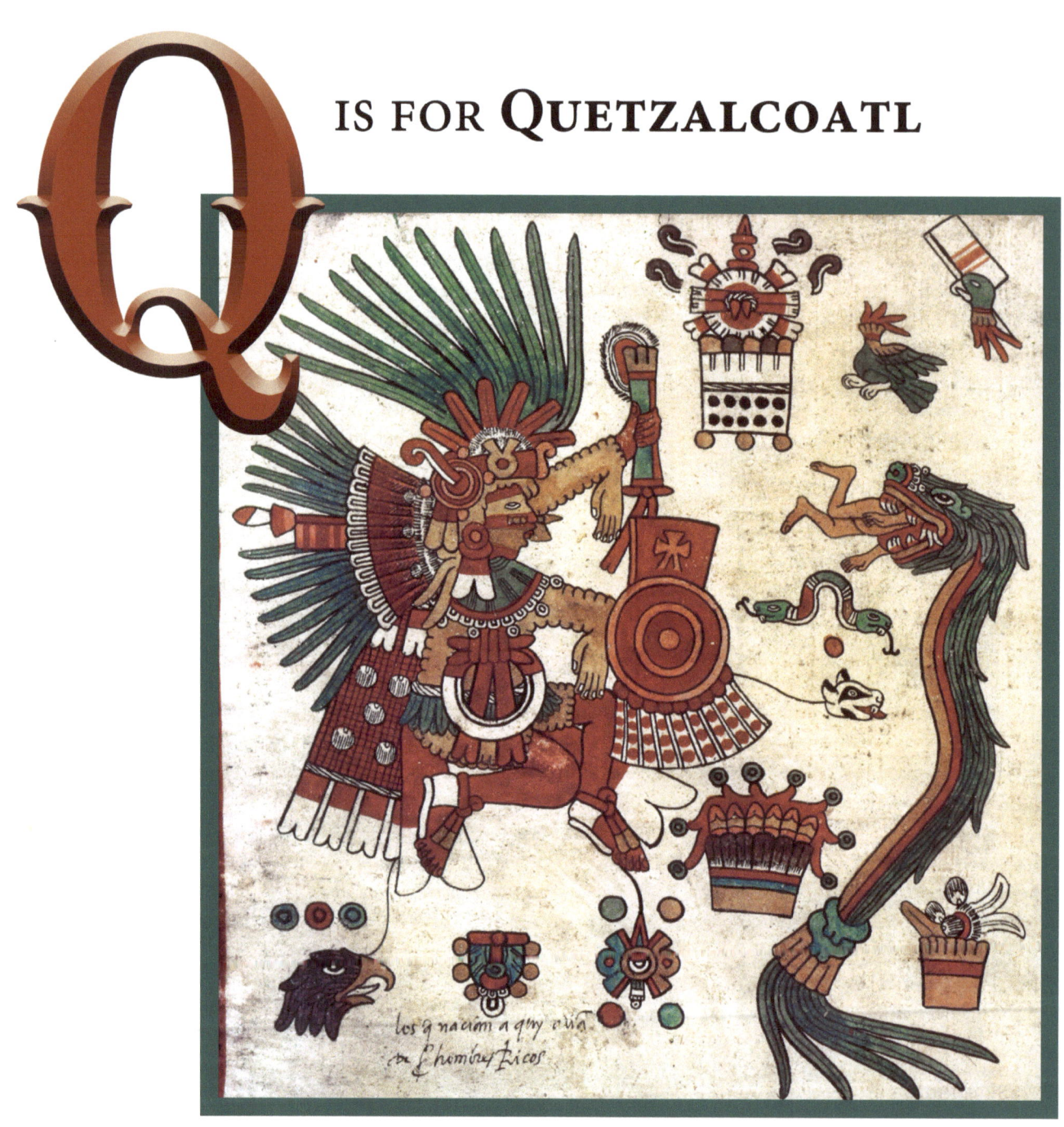

Quetzalcoatl, Ket-sal-kowatl, the Plumed Serpent. Aztec god of the wind and wisdom, maize, patron god of learning and knowledge, instrumental in the creation of the universe, god of intelligence and self-reflection, giver of life. God of merchants, agriculture, arts and crafts, inventor of calendars and books. Originally a vegetation god, symbol of death and resurrection. Many of his titles are acquired through his relationship with other gods in the Aztec pantheon. He shares the planet Venus as the morning star, with Tlahuizcalpanteuctli, the astronomer deity. Tlaloc(the god of rain), an ally of Quetzalcoatl, also represents Venus. It is under the name Ehecatl that Quetzalcoatl is associated with the wind. It is clear that his role was revised and developed over time. He was the third son of Ometecuhtli and Omecihuatl or, the son of the goddess Chimalma, conceived when Mixcoatl shot her with an arrow. With his brother and opposite, Tezcatlipoca, or with their younger brother, Huitzilopochtli, (depending upon which myth you want to believe) he created the cosmos, fire, and the first humans of the 5th epoch. We are now in the 5th epoch of Aztec history, the four previous epochs ended as a result of fighting between Quetzalcoatl and Tezcatlipoca. Tezcatlipoca is in control of this age. It is possible that Quetzalcoatl will return, something the Aztecs were anticipating. This idea gave birth to the story that when Cortés arrived in 1519 by sea in the east, Moctezuma II, the Aztec ruler at the time, thought that Cortés might be Quetzalcoatl. That has been debunked as just that, a story. Other myths have Quetzalcoatl descending to Mictlan, the Aztec underworld, to get some bones he planned to use to create humans. During his escape from Mictlan, he dropped the bones, now slightly out of order, he mixed them with his blood and corn (which he also brought to the Aztec, that's another story) and made the first humans of the 5th age. The Aztecs told this story as a way to explain why people come in different sizes.

Teotihuacan, the archaeological site outside Mexico City was built more than 1000yrs. before the Aztec arrived in the area. The site covered 8 square miles, its builders are unknown but their culture influenced many others throughout Mexico and Central America. Teotihuacan is where the first record is found of a feathered serpent being worshiped. The Temple of the Feathered Serpent is the third largest pyramid at Teotihuacan, its sides are covered with some 260 representations of the feathered serpent. The open mouths of each head is thought to have served as a receptacle for markers that were moved from one to another throughout the year as a means of keeping a ritual calendar.

Cool Fact: *Quetzalcoatlus northropi* a pterosaur discovered in 1971, stood 10 feet tall with a wingspan of at least 36 feet. It is one of the biggest known flying animals of all time. It was found in Big Bend National Park in Texas and is named for John Northrup who pushed for the development of flying wing aircraft. **What other gods' names start with Q?**

R IS FOR **RA, RE**

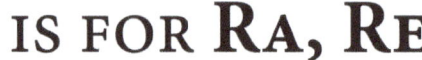

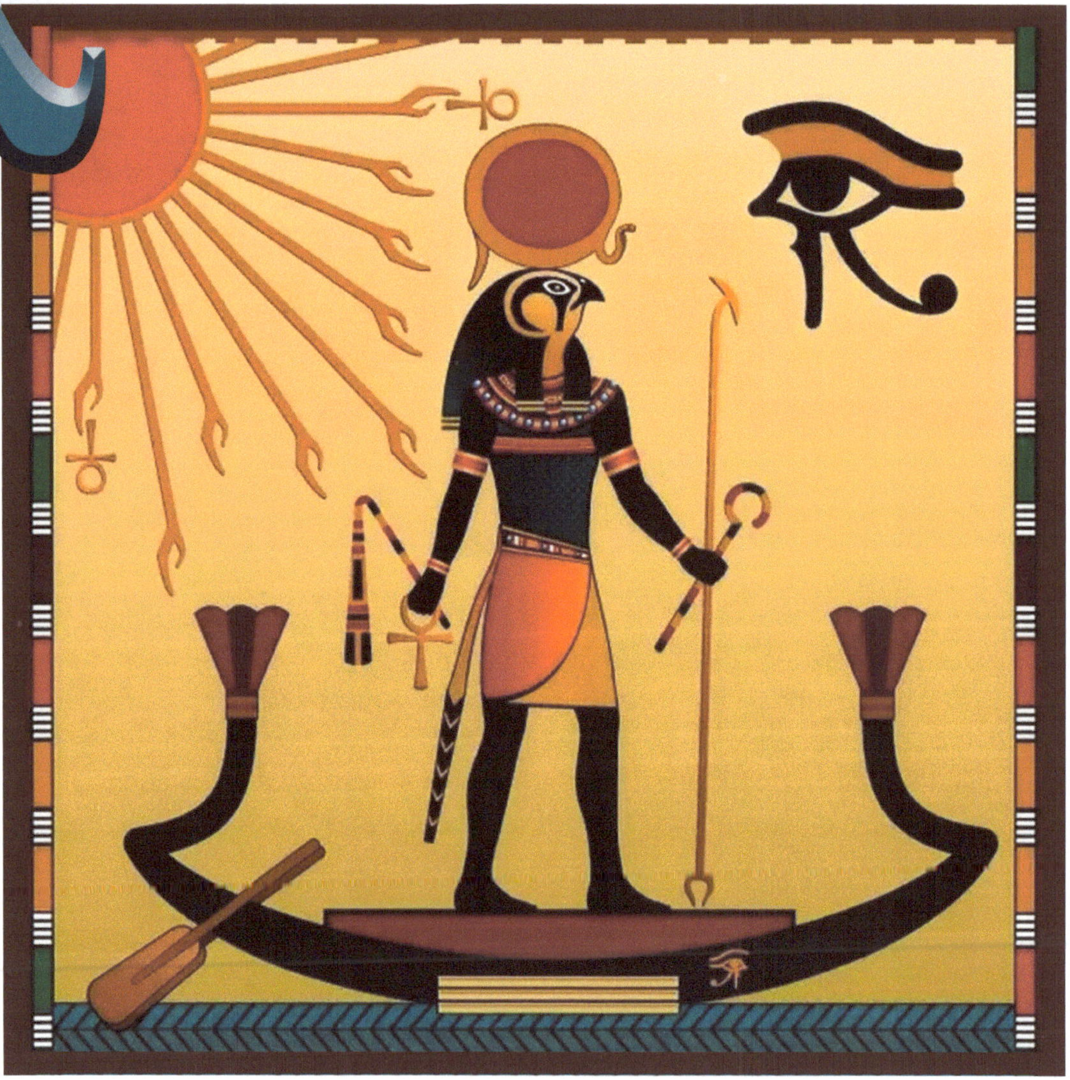

Ra, or **Re** was the Egyptian Sun god who traveled across the sky each day in one boat and went to the underworld each night in his evening boat. Every night, Apophis, the god of chaos, as an enormous serpent, would try to consume the boat or stop it with a hypnotic stare. Sometimes Ra's Ennead (see below) would come to the rescue, other times, by his rising, Ra would represent the rebirth of the sun by the sky goddess Nut. The Great Ennead of Heliopolis, Ra's cult center, consisted of, Shu and Tefnut, deities of air and moisture, who Ra had created, Geb and Nut, representing earth and sky; and Osiris, Isis, Seth and Nephthus. Nine gods (some being no more than another name for Ra at certain times.) Many other groupings were conceived over the centuries, each with its own myths and functions. While Ra was always the Sun God, seen as the giver of life, essential to the ripening of crops, creator of all forms of life, (humans coming from his tears and sweat) he took on more names and guises as time went by. Usually depicted as a man with the head of a falcon under a solar disk encircled by a serpent, he also appeared as a man with a rams head or the head of a beetle, he might also be shown as a phoenix, heron, serpent, bull, cat or lion, to name a few.

Pharaohs started taking on the name "Son of Ra" in the 4th dynasty (c 2575-2465 BCE) the time when the great pyramids were constructed. "Son of Ra" put the Pharaoh up there with the sun god while "Perfect God" (sometimes given as "Good God") meant he had been "perfected" through getting the job of Pharaoh. It's highly unlikely that any one person had a complete grasp of all the mythology surrounding Ra. Religion was a big industry in ancient Egypt, employing many people, including builders, artists and craftsmen, and laborers, not to mention countless priests and their acolytes. The masses had little involvement other than to attend festivals, with little or no knowledge of the workings of the priesthood or royalty. Ignorance is bliss, after all.

Through the centuries Ra remained the most worshiped god, the Roman Empire adopted Christianity as the state religion during the time it occupied and ruled Egypt so, paganism had to go. Not a phenomenon that hadn't happened before in the history of Egypt. So, out went the Sun God, in came the Son of God.

Cool Fact: The 2016 film, *Gods of Egypt* was shot in Australia on a budget of $140million, in it Geoffrey Rush plays Ra. The plot is more complex than the myths created in ancient Egypt, which are hard enough to follow. The film received 5 nominations at the 37th Golden Raspberry Awards.

What other gods' names start with R?

S IS FOR SAHASRANĀMA

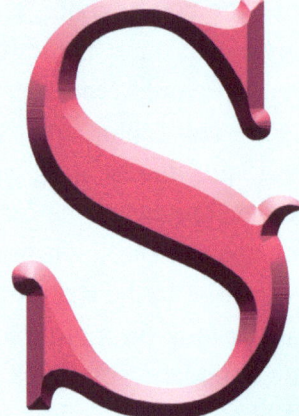

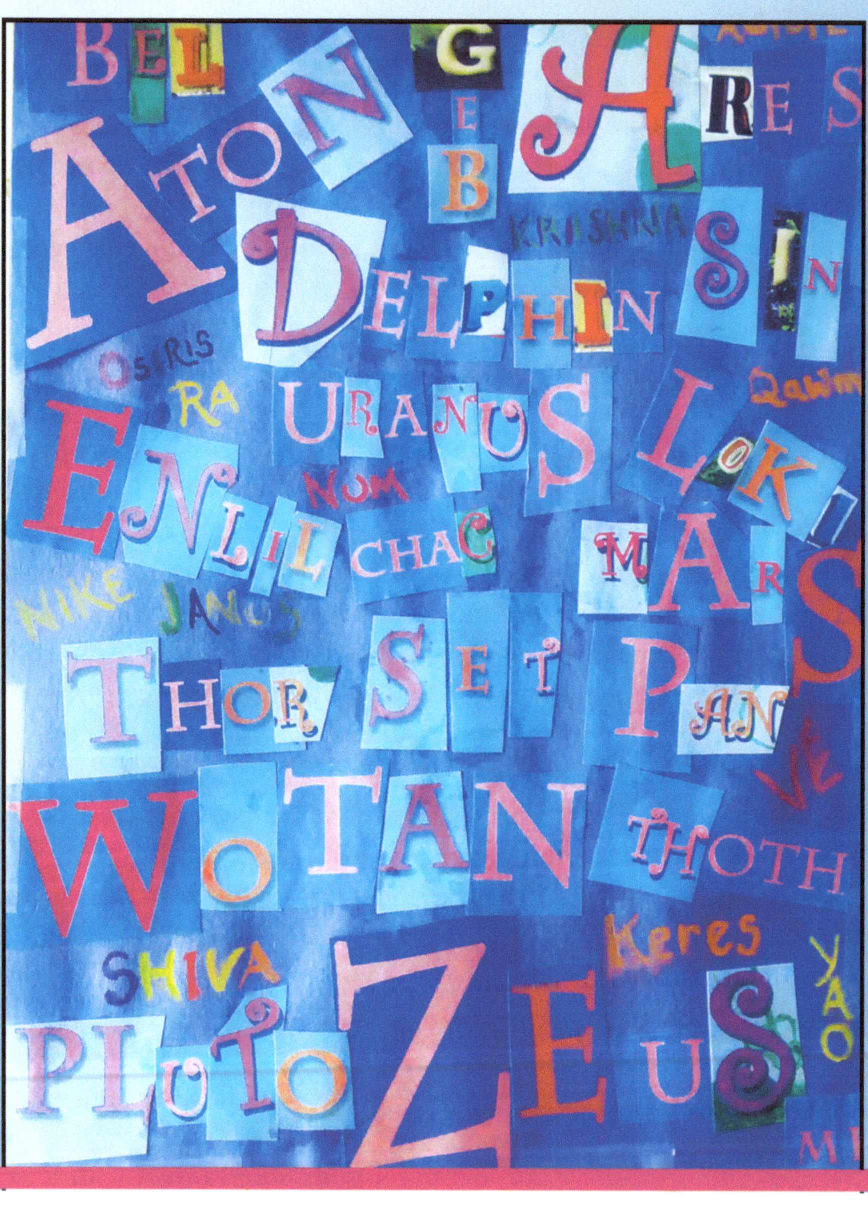

S　**Sahasranāma** in Sanskrit means "1000 names", as *stotras* they are songs of praise. Each Hindu god or goddess may have a thousand names, for instance, there are the Ganesha Sahasranāma and the Lalita Sahasranāma, etc. Each list will contain the names of other gods. The names being the attributes, virtues or energies that those gods embody. The branch of Hinduism called Shaivism is considered the oldest religion in the world. While Brahman is the supreme god, Shaivites focus on Shiva and Vaishnavites worship the incarnations of Vishnu, which includes Rama and Krishna.

Zoroastrians have 101 names of god, Ahura, 'lord', Mazda, 'wisdom' being the first and highest in the pantheon. At one time invoked as a triad that included Mithra, the all-seeing god of truth, and Anahita, goddess of fertility, healing, and wisdom. Founded by Zarathustra, Zoroastrianism is one of the oldest continuously practiced religions. Its written history dates from the 5th century BCE. Religions that were influenced by Zoroastrianism include, Judaism, Christianity, Islam, Buddhism, and also Greek philosophy. The rise of Islam brought about the decline of Zoroastrianism throughout the Middle East, in Armenia its decline was due to Christianity. India now has the largest congregation of Zoroastrians but ex-pat communities are found around the world.

Islam has 99 names for God, some appear in the Qur'an, some in the Hadith, some appear in both but, there is no universal agreement as to what exactly counts as a name of God. Those divine names belong to God alone, however, the addition of "*abd*" (slave or servant) makes them available to male adherents, thus, Abdullah means "Servant of God". For females, the prefix is, *amat*.

Judaism has 7 names for God, they are considered to be so holy once written they cannot be erased. Names such as "Merciful", "Gracious", etc., included in other religions, are considered to represent attributes found in humans and therefore not holy. YHWH or YHVH (you have to provide your own vowels) the name God used to describe himself to Moses is usually written in English as "Yahweh" but since it is forbidden to pronounce that name it is replaced with *Adonai* ("The Lord"). El as a name of God has gotten into humans' names, Daniel ("God's judgment"), Gabriel ("Strength of God"), and Michael ("Who is like God?").

Christianity uses God, The Lord God, or God the Father. A strange theological fight shook the Russian Orthodox Church in the early 20th century. The argument went something like this: one side said, "before Creation, God didn't need a name, so the name was invented and is actually an empty sound with no mystical attributes in and of itself." The other argument, known as the "mystical formula" is; a) the name of God is the energy of God, inseparable from the essence of God itself and therefore is God himself. b) However, God is distinct from his energies and from his name, and that is why God is not his name or a name in general." Believe it or not, Monks on one side of the argument were beaten, imprisoned, defrocked and killed, over the whole thing. Throw in the names of all the gods in the world and you have several Sahasranāma.

Cool Fact: The Golden Arrow prayer goes: May the most holy, most sacred, most adorable, most incomprehensible and ineffable Name of God be forever praised, blessed, loved, adored and glorified in Heaven, on earth, and under the earth, by all the creatures of God.

What other gods' names start with S?

T IS FOR THOR

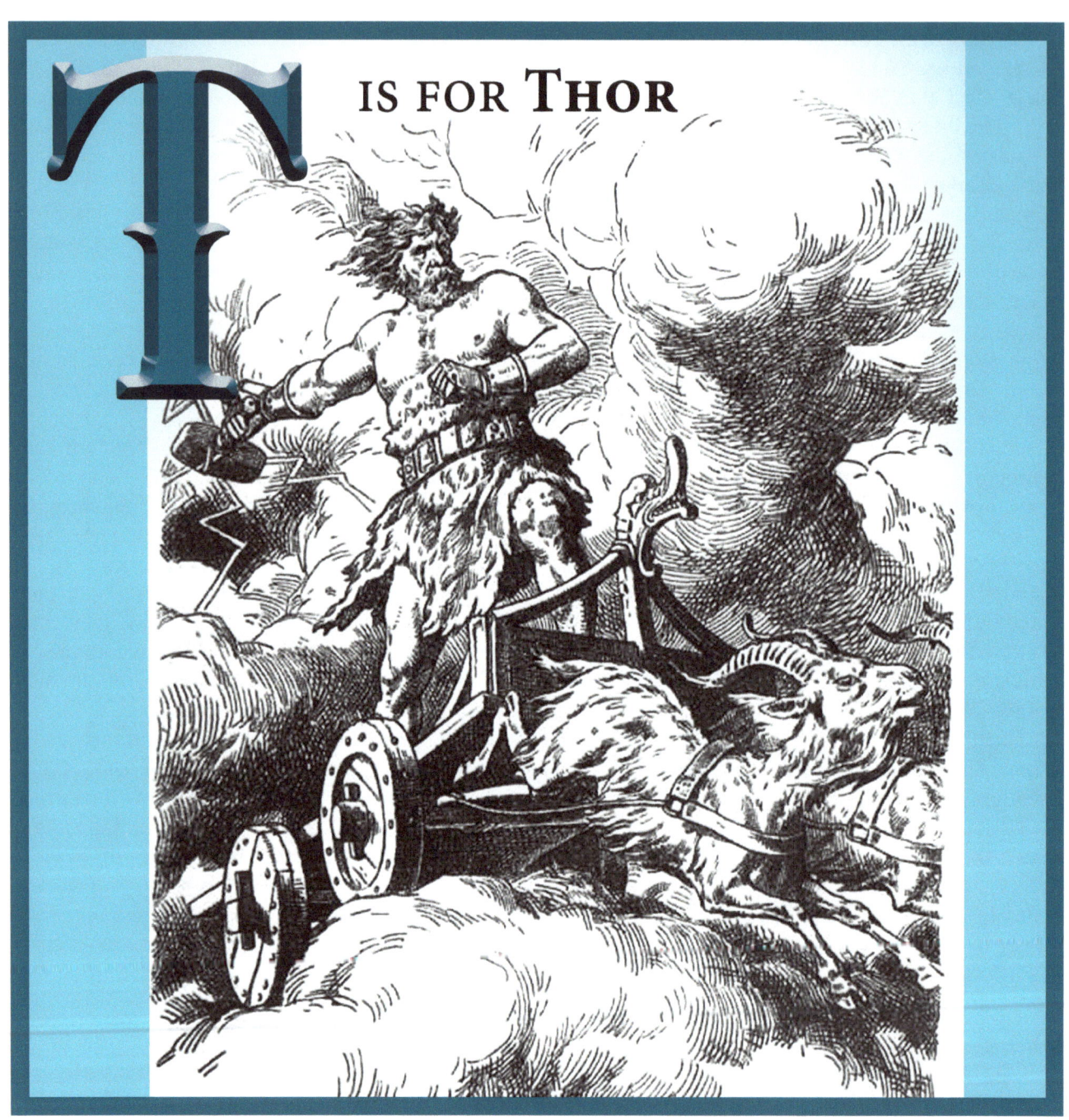

Thor pronounced, torr. The hammer-wielding god of thunder, Thor is well known, thanks to popular entertainment but, who was he really? He was a Norse god and, yes, he had a hammer, capable of leveling mountains with one blow and was associated with thunder and lightning, storms, at sea and on land, sacred groves, strength, and fertility. That sound you hear during a thunderstorm? That's Thor's chariot wheels, you might also hear the hooves of the two goats that pull the chariot. His magic belt doubles his strength and his iron gloves help him wield his hammer.

Thor and Loki spent the night at a farmstead and, as he was wont to do, Thor shared the meat of his goats with the family, (he resurrects the goats the following day) one of the two children of the family sucked the marrow out of one of the leg bones. Sure enough, one of the goats was lame the next day. Thor, who has a reputation for flying off the handle, was so enraged he made the brother and sister his servants. They get to ride in his chariot and accompany him on a number of adventures involving monsters, trolls, and demons. Many of the stories were meant to deliver some lesson or piece of wisdom. The collection of poems known as the **Poetic Edda,** that were usually sung and some of which were acted out, contain stories of Thor and other gods' exploits. Included are the events of Ragnarök, variously translated as, "the twilight of the gods", or "the fate of the gods", etc. tell how all the gods including Thor, die in an epic battle and the world is consumed in fire. Fear not, the earth reappears, the children of the gods survive, Thor's two sons get their father's hammer, and a man and woman who hid in a tree during the whole disaster, repopulate the world. The sun's daughter, at least as beautiful as her mother, will follow her mother's path. Happy ending. Now let's not mess it up again!

Always shown with a red beard and long red hair, Thor was impetuous and impatient, this left him open to deception, and many stories portray him being tricked. While he was tough and a man of action, even housewives would look to him as someone who would help them with their difficulties. Son of Odin and Jöro, the personification of the earth, Thor was the most popular Norse god, his popularity reached its height around c 790-1000CE when Christianity was introduced to Scandinavia. By the 12th century Christianity had replaced the cult of Thor, his temples were torn down and Thor's hammer amulets worn around the neck were replaced with the cross.
Thursday is named for the god Thor.

Cool Fact: A Netflix Norwegian language TV series called Ragnarök takes place in the fictional town of Edda. Climate change and a factory creating terrible pollution are destroying the town. The Jutul family who own the factory, are actually Jötunn, (giants, elves, or trolls). A teenage boy who is the embodiment of Thor, hammer and all, takes on the battle to save the planet from the Jötunn's destructive ways.

What other gods' names start with T?

U IS FOR Ulanji

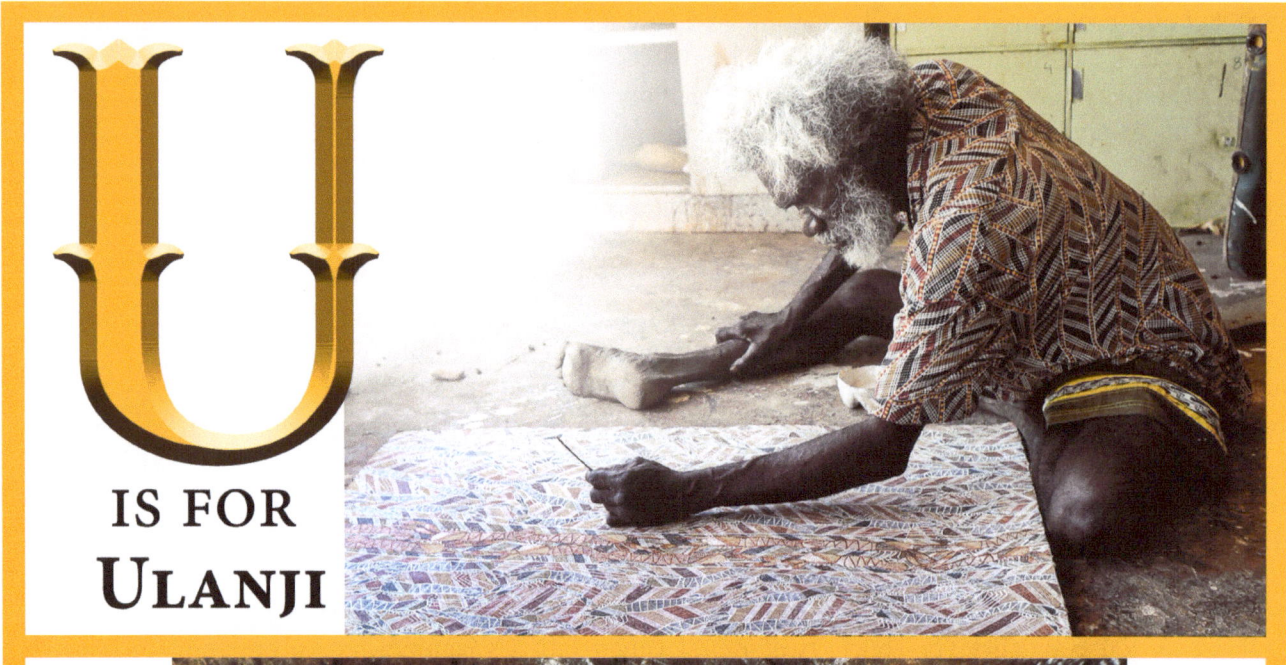

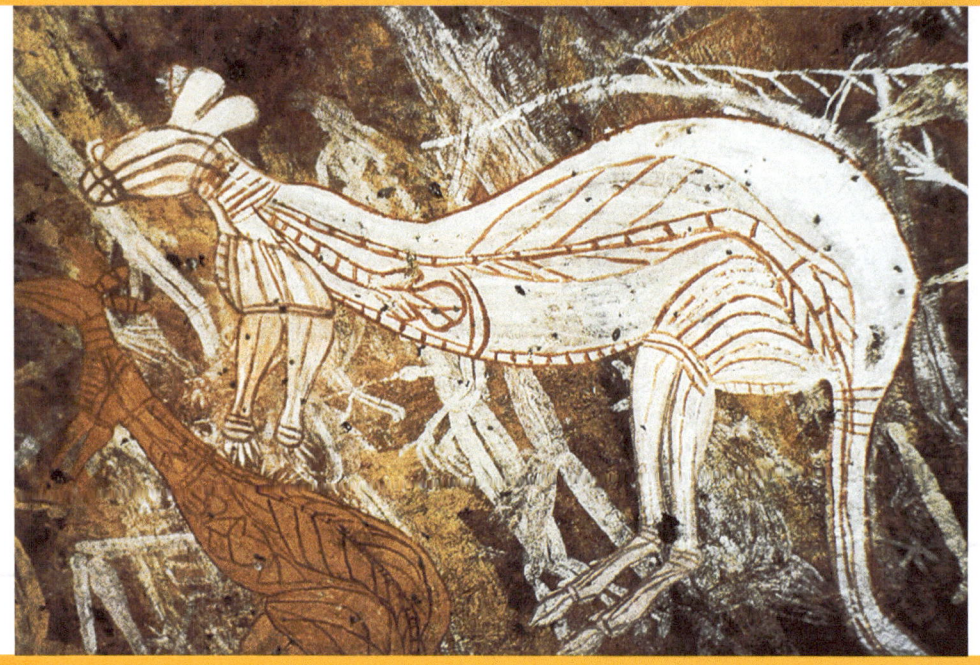

U **Ulanji**, snake ancestor of the Binbinga, or Binbinka, indigenous people of the Northern Territory of Australia. Their traditional lands of some 4,400 sq. miles encompass the McArthur river where they camped in their *mia-mias,* shelters of branches, bark, leaves, and grass. The Binbinga are one of the 900 distinct Aboriginal groups of Australia, each with its own language or dialect. Each with its own set of stories that are often similar, having been told, performed, and developed over thousands of years. The mythical elements of these stories include descriptions of places and events of the past that have proven to be accurate geographically and historically. Such as the formation of coastlines, mountains, and lakes that occurred up to 10,000 years ago. The performance of these stories provide a link to the past and a way to relate to their environment. Most of these stories take place in the Dreamtime, the time of creation, the distant past that is accessible through the medium of the story-telling process. Chanting, dancing, and the playing of the didgeridoo and percussive sticks create the sought for transformative atmosphere. Ulanji, sometimes called a god, other times a supernatural being, lived in the Dreamtime, he was a huge snake that emerged from a hole in the ground called Makumundana, there he made a water-hole filled with water lilies. As he moved across the land he created springs and creeks and a river, he made hills and mountain ranges. He conducted ceremonies on each of these occasions, at which time spirit-children sprang from his body to inhabit each of the locations. At one site, Kunella-dat-Kaula, he found flying foxes (fruit-eating bats) hanging from rocks, he decapitated them. He took two of his ribs, shaped them into trees, and planted them. At Tutita he left quartzite for the fashioning of knives and spearheads. At another place, Nanawandula, he made water-holes filled with crocodiles. There he removed his heart, changing the name of the place to, Kurto-Lula, heart. He then sank underground, traveled to the end of his journey, Uminiwura, where he emerged only to disappear again into the earth. Of the nearly 100 Australian gods only one other's name starts with U: Ungod, another snake deity, associated with fertility and erections of tribal shamans.

Like the indigenous people of the Americas and elsewhere, Australian aborigines suffered the loss of their lands, their cultures and the impact of the alien ways of those that arrived from the other side of the world. Those that choose to integrate do so with varied results, those that continue to live as their ancestors did, must do so within the laws of the predominantly white majority. Appreciation of their arts and culture is growing and a clearer understanding of their approach to the environment is bringing about changes for the better. On February 13th, 2008 Australia's Prime Minister formally apologized to the Aboriginal population for the laws and policies of successive governments that adversely impacted their lives and those of their parents and grandparents. The members of the "Stolen Generation," mostly bi-racial children who were separated from their parents, families and communities received additional apologies for the pain and suffering they endured.

Cool Fact: The didgeridoo is traditionally made from the trunk or root of a eucalyptus tree that has been hollowed out by termites. The bark is removed, the inside cleaned out, then painted with the player's personal images, it is ready to play. The player usually maintains a continuous tone through circular breathing while moving his lips to keep time and rhythm. PVC pipe has been found to work well too.

What other gods' names start with U?

V

IS FOR
**Velnias,
Velinas,
Vels**

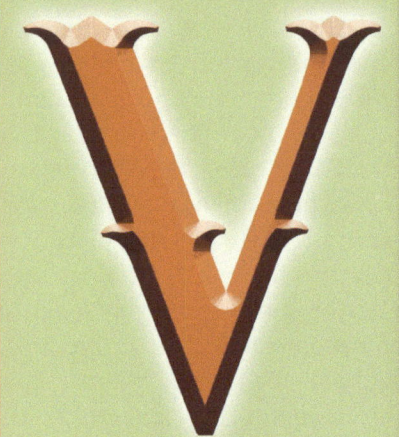

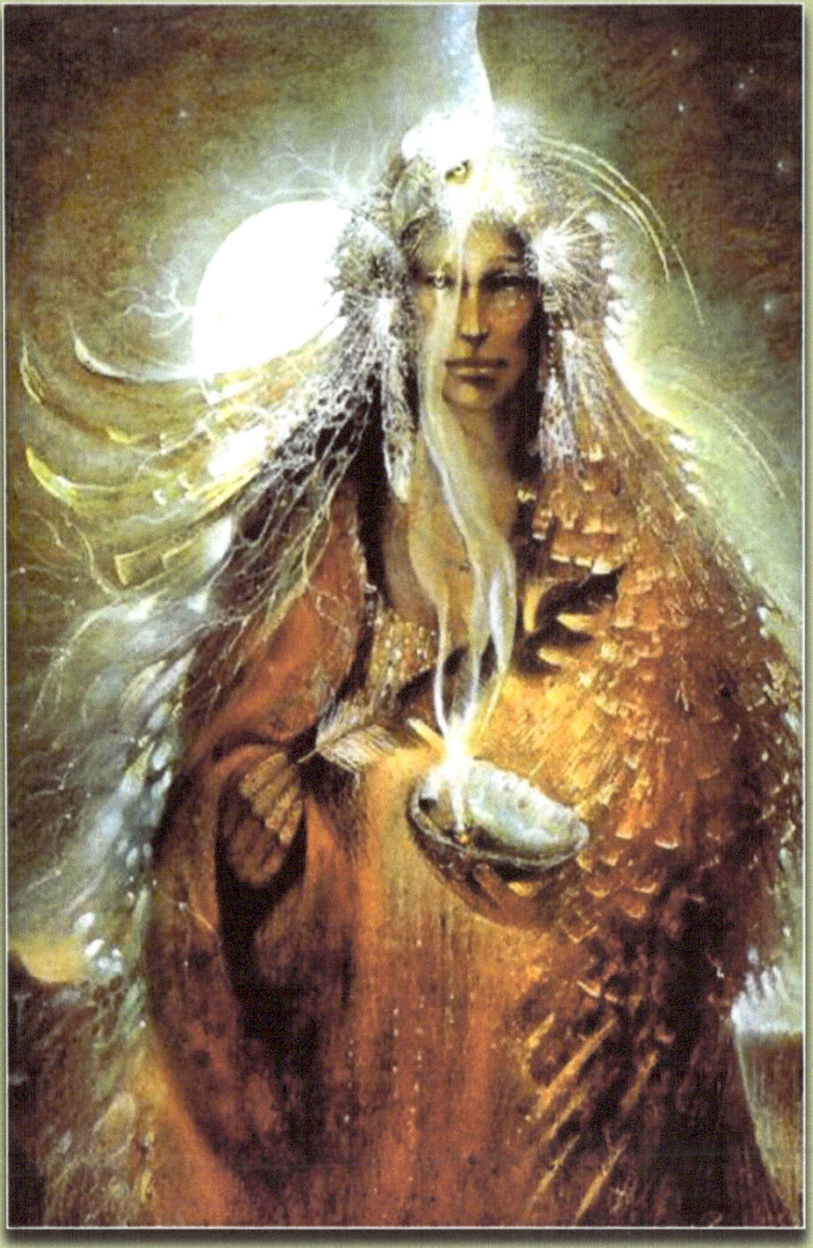

Velnias, Lithuanian god of death and rebirth, a one-eyed, prophetic trickster, the "phantom of the dead." Velnias and his brother Dievas co-created the earth. Dievas tricked Velnias into getting a piece of soil from the bottom of the ocean, he gives the soil to Dievas who spreads it on the water where it continues to spread. The dirt left in Velnias' mouth, (that was the only way he could carry it) also spreads and he coughs it up, creating the rough surface of the earth, lakes, and rocks. Just one example of the collaboration and competition between the brothers. Dievas then is the Sky Father, he makes the sun, grass, birds, he is the creator of humans, cultural values, legislated law and order. He could turn himself into an old man and go from village to village and house to house giving presents and helping people. Velnias is the Swamp Father, he makes all the creepy crawly things, all the harmful animals, all the bad, disorderly, and damaging things that happen. He is associated with moors, swamps, and lakes; pools of water being seen as routes to the underworld, the realm of the dead. He may live under the earth but he also flies through the air during storms, leading the spirits of the dead, causing storms and whirlwinds. This puts him in direct conflict with Perkūnas, god of thunder who carries out the will of Dievas. Associated with trade, hunting, and agriculture, Velnias too can shape-shift, appearing as animals, birds, reptiles, and people of all different ages and professions, helping people in their work but also tempting and mocking them and sometimes doing them harm. Physically attractive, he is always seeking love and sometimes, marriage. His connection to death and reincarnation dates to prehistoric times and ancestor worship. As the guardian of the dead, he goes to funerals to take the soul of the dead person. In the old Indo-European tradition, musicians and poets were associated with magicians, wizards, and witchcraft, those inspired by the outer world, the world of the dead. When Christianity came along Velnias was equated with the devil, becoming the god of evil, the underworld, underground wealth, and dead animals.

Baltic, Slavic and Celtic mythology, through time, influenced each other, just as people moved through the land influencing and being influenced in their turn, so we see any number of variations and contradictions in the names and functions of the gods. Equated with a number of other gods and other names, nevertheless, in spite of it all, or perhaps because of, Velnias is the most popular god in Lithuanian folklore.

Cool Fact: Lithuanian *vèles* and Latvian *velis* mean, "Zombie."

What other gods' names start with V?

W IS FOR **Wulbari**

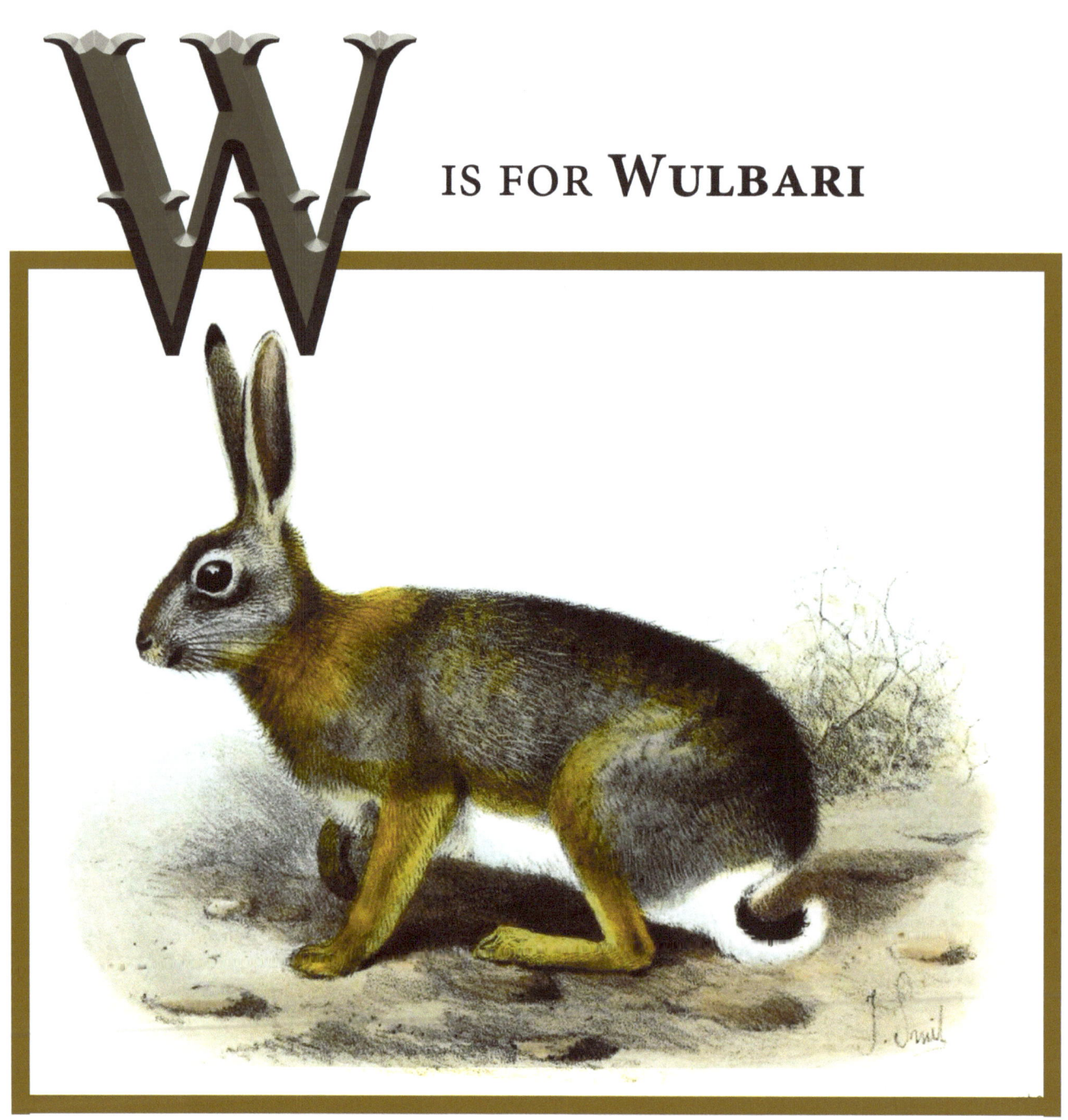

Wulbari, Creator God of the Krachi people of Togo, W. Africa was heaven itself dwelling just above Asase Y, the earth goddess. People living on earth kept bumping their heads on Wulbari which upset him. Smoke from an old woman's cooking fire got in his eyes and her stirring pole kept poking him, upsetting him even more. So he raised heaven up a little higher. People began to use the heavenly blue as a towel to wipe their dirty hands and one woman took a piece of the blue to add to her soup. Annoyed, Wulbari moved higher and higher till he was the heaven we see today. This is how and why God who originally was on earth, became more and more detached from the lives of people. The Bantu creator god, Mulungu, shares a similar story. In his, he asks Spider to weave a web for him to climb higher. In heaven, Wulbari set up his court which was made up of all the animals, headed by their captain, and Wulbari's guard, Anansi, Spider. Anansi was the trickster, a character we find in many mythologies. The trickster's job is to speak truth to power, to deflate the ego of those that have a high opinion of themselves, and to make fools of them. When Anansi boasted that he had more sense than god, Wulbari called him in and told him to go find *something* and bring it to him, convinced that Anansi would never figure out what that *something* was. Disguising himself in a cloak made from feathers all the birds gave him, Anansi sat on a branch of a tree by Wulbari's house. Wulbari asked all the animal people what kind of bird it was but nobody knew. Someone suggested Anansi might know but Wulbari told them he had sent him off to find *something*. 'What something?' they asked. When Wulbari told them the *something* was the sun, the moon, and the darkness, Anansi took off to find them. He put them in a sack and took them to Wulbari. People who looked directly at the sun when it was pulled from the sack were blinded, that is why there is blindness in the world. By his quick-wittedness and trickery, Anansi proved himself equal to god.

Africans brought to this country as slaves could draw upon trickster tales in order to survive. One might act too dumb to be trusted with the job of picking cotton, tobacco, or cutting sugar cane in order to be given the easier task of feeding chickens or clearing trash. Another might prove how quick and bright he was, in order to obtain a place in the Plantation House as a butler, making use of the opportunities that position offered. In African folklore, the savanna hare appears in many trickster tales, its American descendant, Br'er Rabbit, is an example of how the trickster could overcome injustice and thrive. Through such characters, slaves, though forced to speak English, communicated with each other in ways their masters were unable to comprehend.

Cool Fact: A crater on Rhea, the second-largest moon of Saturn, is named Wulbari.
What other gods' names start with W?

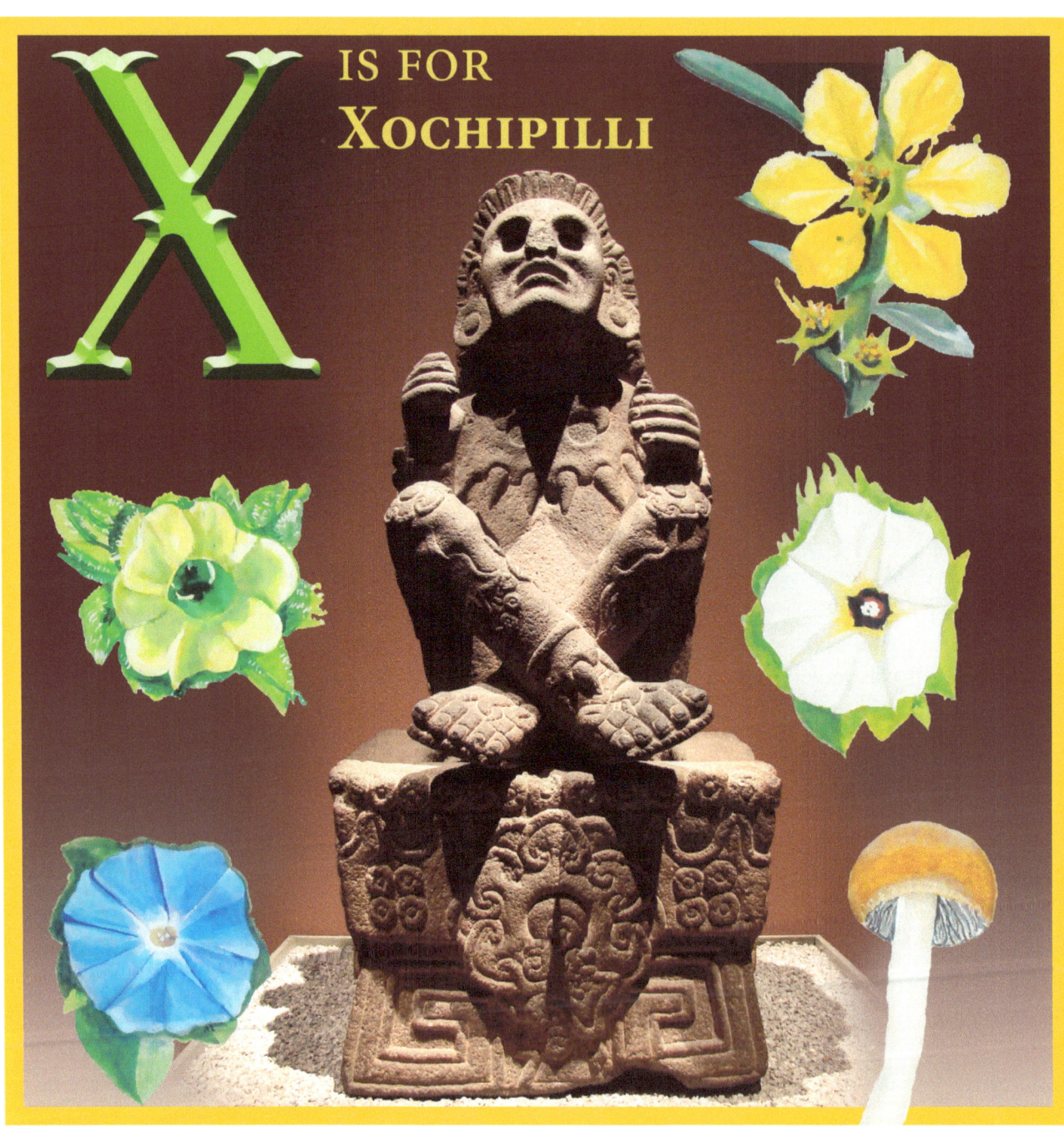

X **Xochipilli**. Xochitl- Flower, pilli- prince or child. Flower Prince or Flower Child. Long before the summer of Love, this flower child, his brothers, Ixtlilton, god of health, medicine, and dancing, and Machilxochitl, god of games, and his soul sister, Xochiquetzal kept people happy and healthy. A welcome change from all those angry vengeful Gods. He was the God of Spring, Flowers, Feasting, Love, Music, Song, and Dance, Creativity, and Souls, linked to agriculture and staples like Maize. He may have been absorbed from the Toltec, as many other Aztec things were. As such he has also been seen as the patron god of homosexuals and male prostitutes; his sister watched over female prostitutes. He was capable of lighthearted mischief and practical jokes but, he wasn't a *trickster*, they can get malicious at times. He was popular and beloved. The annual summer Festival of Flowers honored Xochipilli and Xochiquetzal. During the festival pulque was drunk and psychedelic mushrooms were eaten. No human sacrifices at this one, only a good time for all. A statue found on the western slopes of Popocatepetl and Iztacoihuatl, now in the Museum of Anthropology and History, in Mexico City, shows Xochipilli totally absorbed in temicxoch, the 'flowery dream.' In Nahuatl poetry, "flowers," "flowering" and "dream flowers" refer to the state induced by the hallucinogenic plants and mushrooms shown on the sculpture. These "flowers" took the user to the world they called Tlalocan, "a wonderous world where they reveled in sensations beyond imagining." So wrote Robert Gordon Wasson (1898-1986) in his book, *The Wonderous Mushroom- Mycology in Mesoamerica.*

The Aztec believed that Xochipilli was originally a mortal married to a girl named Mayahuel, that together they discovered the joys of intoxicating drink. They introduced it to the gods who were so delighted, they granted the couple divinity. Mayahuel became the goddess of pulque. This is just one of the stories about the discovery of pulque. Made from the fermenting sap of the maguey, (the Century Plant) or agave, pulque, together with mescal and tequila and the lesser-known, bacanora and raicilla, all made from some part of the maguey, were the most popular alcoholic drinks available in Mexico before the introduction of beer from Europe. Pulque lost its popularity and became associated with the poor and dissolute. Recently it is having some success as a health food due to its supposed nutritional value. There is a saying about pulque, "solo le falta un grado para ser carne." "it is only a bit shy of being meat." Xochipilli would be proud, I'm sure.

Cool Fact: The Oregon Psilocybin Services Act was approved as a ballot measure in November, 2020. In March 2021, the state's governor announced the members of the newly formed Psilocybin Advisory Board. Psychedelic therapy is being reexamined with trials underway. Previous tests held elsewhere, have shown that participants from the very sick to the "healthy-normal" reported profound changes in their outlook. It could be life-changing for those with mental health problems.

What other gods' names start with X?

Y is for Yurupari

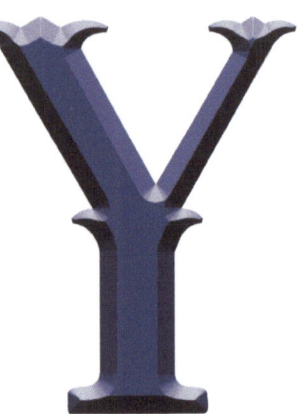

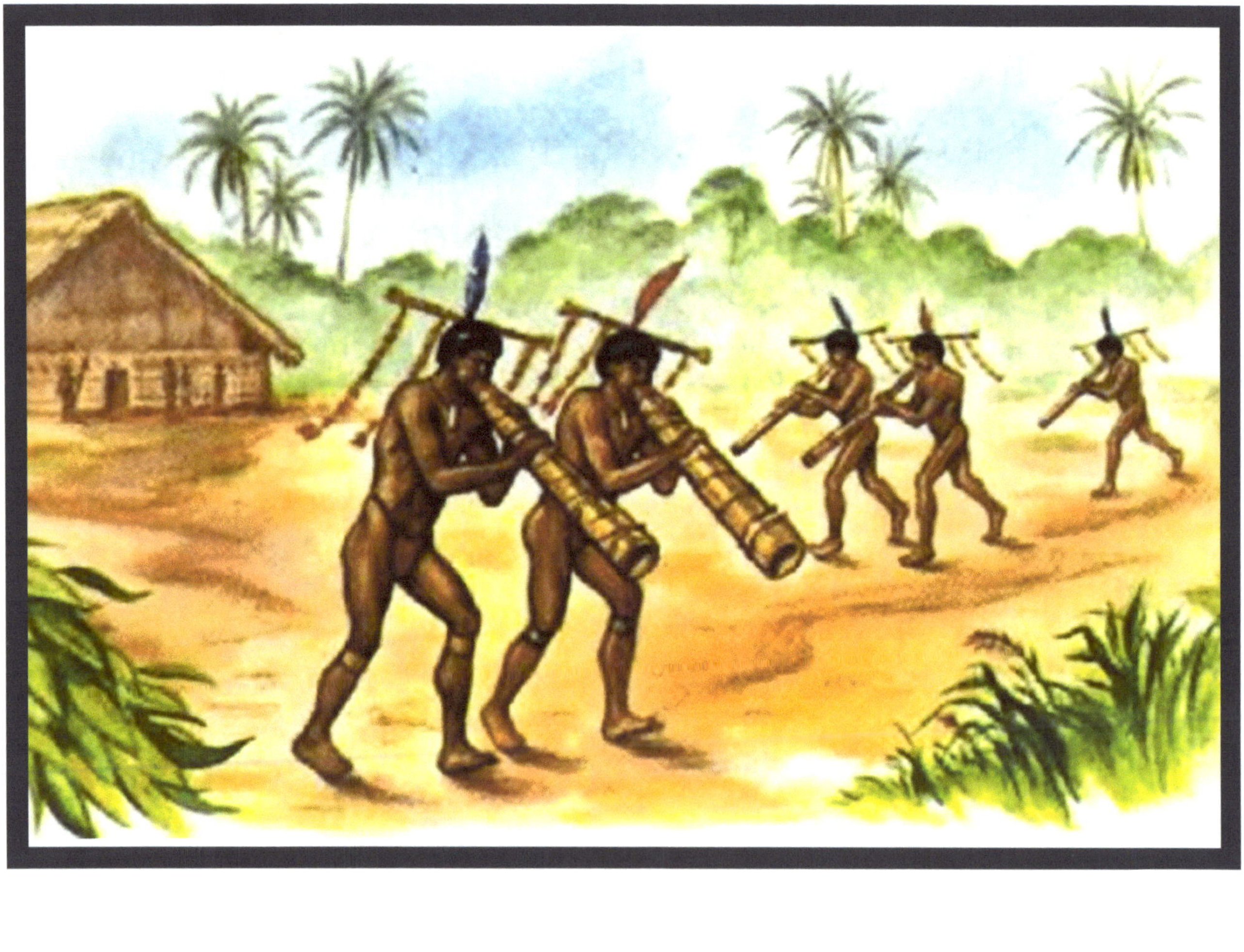

Yurupari, is it a god? Is it a cult? No! Its Yurupari! One anthropologist said that Yurupari in the Tupi language means "secret mystery" another said it derives from the Geral language. It is associated with the "trumpets" which produce "Yurupari" music, to another. Yurupari is the ancestor god of the Indians of the Amazon Basin in Brazil or, an ancestor cult complex. First associated with the Arawak People it is a complex that includes myths and rites of initiation of males among Amazon Basin tribes. To another, Yurupari is a plant demon who makes fruit ripen. For some missionaries, it was a diabolical cult. It can only be understood within the Yucuna culture from the Colombian Amazon, contends one anthropologist. So let's go there. The Yucuna build Malochas, thatched houses with steep roofs, only certain members of the tribe can have a malocha, they must know how to "manage" it, they must know the tribal mythology and rituals. Big malochas are owned by the shamans of the tribe. Divided into three parts, the center of the house is used for ritual celebrations, the final dance of the Yurupari celebrations is held there. The second part is for everyday activities, the third is reserved for the private use of the family. The levels of the roof are a model of the cosmos. There is the level of the heaven of the jungle, the great owner of the animals, the heaven of music, the heaven of the four immortal ancestors, and the heaven of Tupano(a supernatural being.) Drawing on the writings of several anthropologists and one that participated in a Yurupani ceremony, the following becomes clear; there is no one definitive story. The Yurupari myth is reserved for men, it is not spoken about in the presence of women or children or anyone who has not participated in the celebration. Basically, it's a male initiation rite that is held annually between January and March when the umari (*Pouraqueiba paraensis*) fruit is ripe. A four-day event when plenty of coca is taken, plenty of tobacco smoked, there is much vomiting, brought on by the ingestion of ayahuasca, much time spent in the water which helps the initiates to learn how to play the Yurupari flutes, after the shamans have shown them the basics. Several other instruments are played during the ceremony. Novices are taught the historical origins of men's power in their society, Yurupani is invoked in order to communicate with the ancestors and to renew the shared beliefs and myths. Some members participate several times in order to learn more about plants, animals, fish, birds, weather and healing. Yurupari is the generator of vegetable growth, he is the "Sun." For some tribes, Yuruparis are cultural heroes who created insects, reptiles, mosquitoes and gnats, snakes, and poisonous spiders. Several lengthy and complex stories tell of Yurupari's arrival from heaven, how he killed all those that didn't obey him, how he was killed by fire, the only thing that could destroy him, but how he is resurrected the next day as he lives forever. Yurupari remains an important symbol for maintaining the status of men over women and the need to maintain the gender distinctions of the Yucuna society. "It's a man's world! But it wouldn't be nothing, nothing without a woman or a girl." James Brown (1933-2006)

Cool Fact: To keep up with the times, where once Yurupari arrived in a canoe, he now comes in a launch with his tape recorder or, perhaps more recently, with his tablet.

What other gods' names start with Y?

Z IS FOR ZEUS

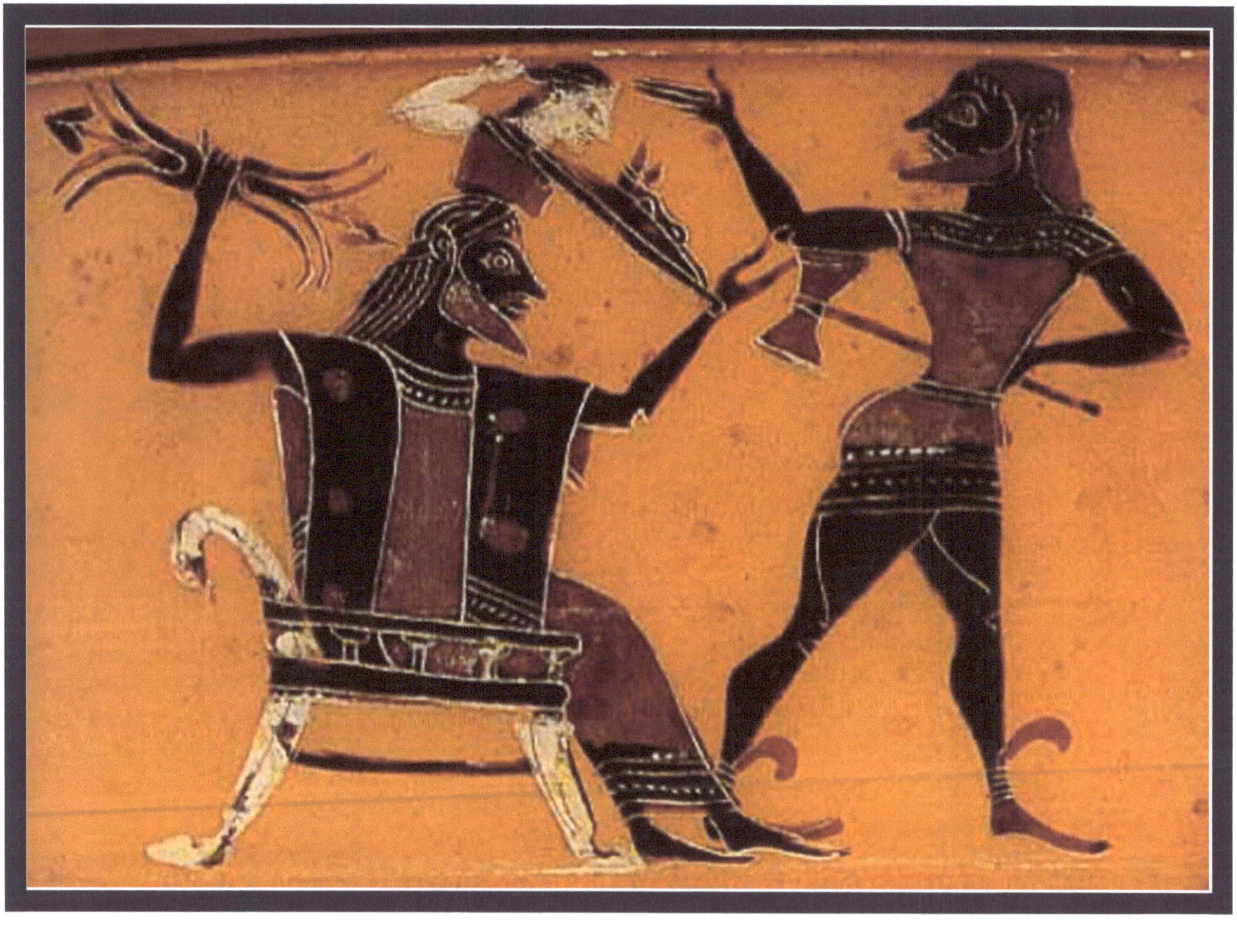

Z Zeus, king of the gods of Mt. Olympus, sky god, god of thunder. His name is related to the earlier Indo-European god Dyeus, from the root meaning "sky" or "shine." He was the youngest son of Cronos and Rhea. Having heard that one of his children would dethrone him, Cronos took the precaution of swallowing each as they were born. When Rhea delivered Zeus she wrapped a stone in a blanket and gave that to Cronos and hid Zeus in a cave. Cronos swallowed the stone. Sure enough, when fully grown, Zeus got Cronos to throw up his siblings, and the stone. Together with Cyclops, who gave Zeus lightning bolts, and the Hekatonkheires, who threw volleys of boulders at the Titans, Zeus and his siblings, now fully grown, defeated Cronos and the Titans, most of whom he imprisoned in the underworld of Tartarus. To the victors go the spoils, as they say, brother Poseidon received the sea, Hades, the underworld, Zeus got the sky together with supreme authority of the earth, including Mt. Olympus. The goddess Metis who had helped Zeus by giving Cronos the magical draught that made him vomit didn't fare so well, learning that she was pregnant and that a son of his would replace him as king of the gods, Zeus swallowed her. Like father, like son. As it happened, she was pregnant with a girl, who was born in Zeus' belly and birthed directly from his head. Athena was her name and she gave Zeus problems for the rest of their lives. After seducing her as a cuckoo, Zeus married his sister Hera, who had grown up to be the most beautiful of the goddesses. He loved her for 300 yrs, although they argued a lot, (he had seduced a number of goddesses, countless nymphs, and women already, with more to come) they had three children. One argument was about who enjoyed sex more, men or women. They put the question to Teiresias, on a scale of ten, he said, women enjoyed it nine times to men's one. With that, Hera blinded him and Zeus gave him the power of prophecy.

The bad behavior of mankind and their practice of human sacrifice horrified Zeus so, he decided to wipe them out. With Poseidon, he flooded the world. As with most flood stories, one couple survived, in this case, Deucalion and Pyrrha with their daughter, Oceanus. On the advice of an Oracle, they threw rocks over their shoulders. His rocks became men, hers became women. So, back where we started. How does it go, the fire next time?

Stories about the gods of Olympus abound, the characters and their stories influenced other civilizations and religions, particularly the Romans who, in most cases, simply changed the gods' names while retaining their attributes. Did Zeus die? There are differing opinions on that. Greek mythology died, along with most other religions' tales as people found something else to believe.

Cool Fact: Metis, goddess of wisdom, took up residence in the stomach of Zeus and continued to exist there. The ancient Greeks believed that the belly, not the brain was the seat of thought and emotion, so from there she provided wise counsel.

What other gods' names start with Z?

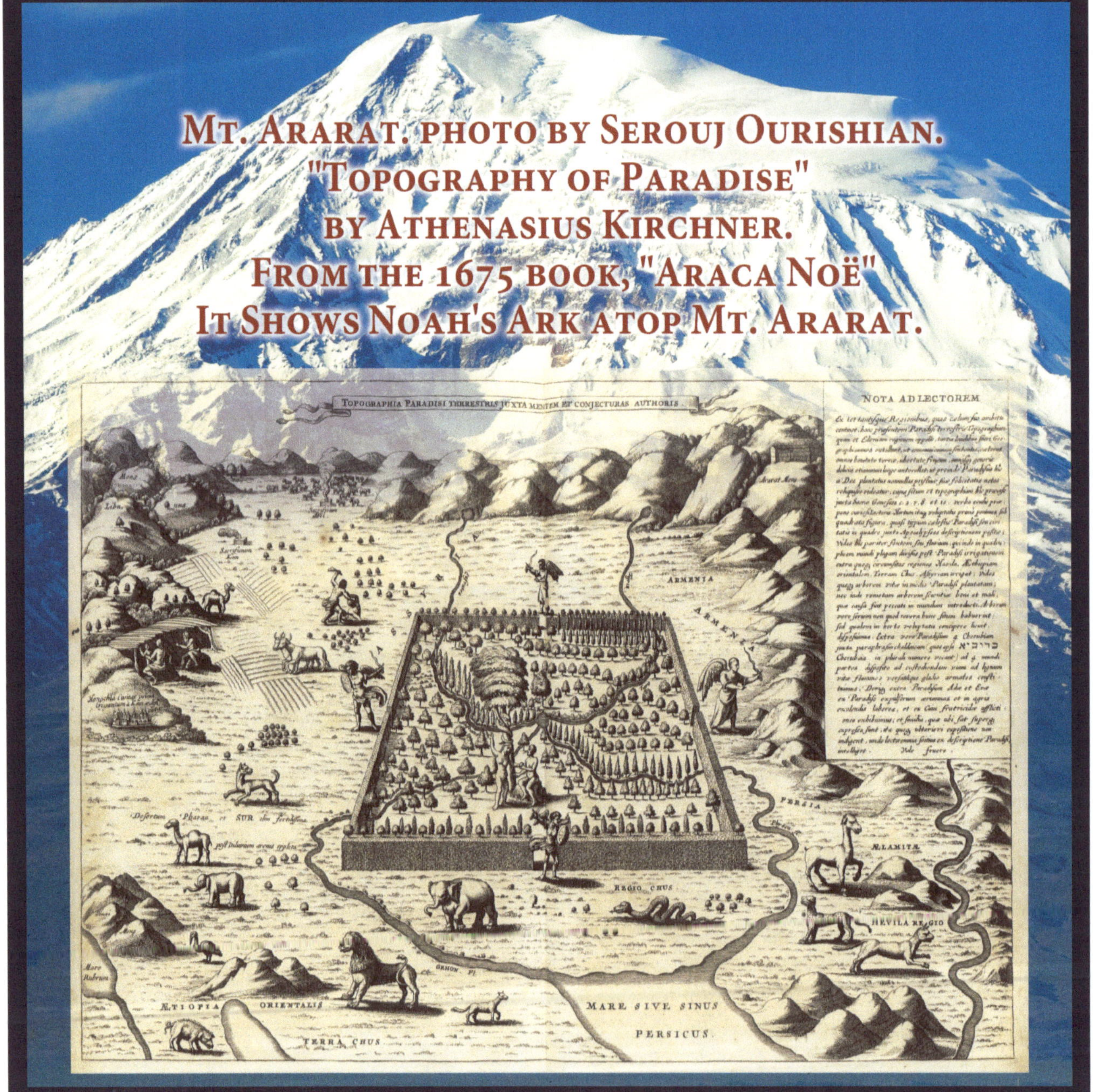

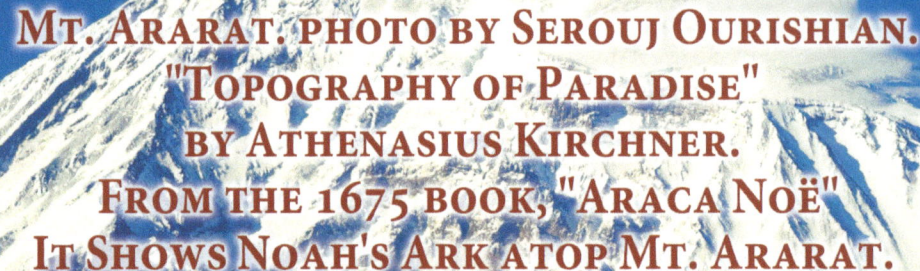

Mt. Ararat. photo by Serouj Ourishian.
"Topography of Paradise"
by Athenasius Kirchner.
From the 1675 book, "Araca Noë"
It Shows Noah's Ark atop Mt. Ararat.

Bonus

Monotheism.

"Thou shalt have no other god before me." This was the message the God of the Hebrews sent. His People were still looking at options like the Golden Calf, so it was necessary while acknowledging there were other gods, he make it clear there were consequences for straying. Establishing a tribe, a People distinct from other people takes time and effort. Having your own god who cares more about you than all those others, is a distinct advantage. Rules and regulations the leaders' setup then have the divine backing of the Lord. The penalties for disobeying are severe, swift and often, deadly. The Lord God of Israel was determined to keep his People in line. Around 2,000yrs. ago, the Roman Empire ruled most of the Middle East, under them the Hebrews were having a hard time, the idea of a Messiah (a descendant of King David) who would lead them out of oppression, had been around for a long time, under these circumstances would-be leaders, claiming to be the Messiah, assumed the mantle. One, Jesus of Nazareth, caught the attention of the Romans, Caesar's mother converted and her son made Christianity the national religion. The other Semitic people in the area felt left out. Luckily, an illiterate trader, while sleeping in a cave, was visited by the angel Gabriel who told him that Allah, god in Arabic, had chosen him, Muhammad, to be his messenger. Drawing on memory, Muhammad dictated to his wife the message that, together with later additions, became the Qur'an. Although it wasn't until after the schism splitting Islam into the Sunni and Shia, shortly after Mohammad's death, that the various texts were unified and transcribed into one. Similar to what happened with the New Testament of Christianity. These three monotheistic religions, acknowledging one god under different names, Yahweh, God and Allah, (the use of either one of them being fraught with problems) are now dominant. None are monolithic; aside from the Sunni, Shia split, other factions abound in Islam. Judaism has orthodox and unorthodox. Christianity split into Roman Catholic, Greek Orthodox, the Church of England and Protestantism; for forty years there was a pope in Rome and one in Avignon, France. Martin Luther,(1483-1546) a German priest, was so appalled by the behavior of the pope and his minions when he visited Rome that he wrote a manifesto which led to the Reformation and started Protestantism which, in time, split into the many forms we have today.

During WWII millions of Jews were killed by the Nazis with the encouragement of a pro-Nazi pope. At the same time the forces of the Emperor God of Japan were killing as many people as they could.

After the USA dropped atom bombs on Japan the Emperor gave up his divinity. The end of the war brought sympathy for the Jews they had not previously known; Israel was created as a home for Jews with the help of a Christian England. The Palestinians, whose land was taken for this, must have wondered what they had done for Allah to allow such a thing. Throughout their history, the three great religions condemned anyone calling into question their dogma. But murder carried out in the name of a religion, that is committed without condemnation by leaders of the faith, who presume to represent god, can only be looked upon as the very nadir of religion. Maintaining the faith is essential not only to preserving the religion but also to the continuation of the gods. The followers of any number of faiths offer their prayers to an All Mighty, who they hope to join in heaven, while others pray their spirit will go to Summerland, the heaven of Spiritualism. Peace on earth, goodwill to all men.

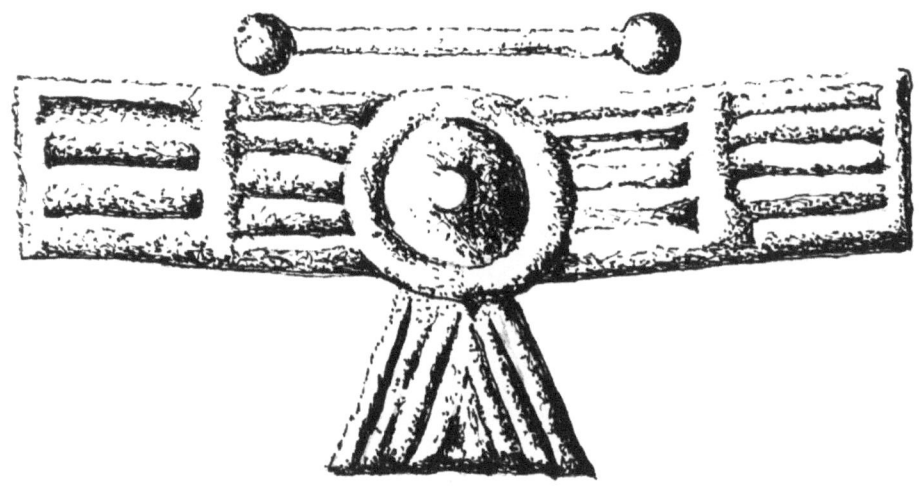

Other god names.

A. Anu, Anunnaki, Apollo, Atlas, Ares
B. Balder, Bragi, Boreas
C. Cronus, Cadmus, Crius
D. Dionysus, Delphin, Dagon, Dagur
E. Eros, Enlil, Ehecatl
F. Februus, Fa, Faro, Favonius
G. Geb, Great Spirit
H. Horus, Hunab, Hermes, Hathor
I. Itzamna, Iapetus, Inti
J. Janus, Jupiter
K. Keres, Kothar, Kitchi Manitou, Khnum
L. Loki, Laertus, Legba
M. Mars, Moloch, Mercury
N. Nirritih, Nun, Nike, Nephthys
O. Osiris, Orcus, Odin, O-Kuni-nushi
P. Pluto, Poseidon, Prometheus, Piltzintli
Q. Quaoar, Quirinius, Qaholom, Qawm
R. Radamanthus,
S. Set, Shamash, Sin, Soma, Seth, Sacsayhuaman
T. Tlaloc, Tartarus, Thoth, Tezcatlipoca
U. Uranus, Utu, Utakh, Umuh
V. Varuna, Viracocha, Veive
W. Wotan, Waag
X. Xipe Totec, Xolotl, Xanthus
Y. Yama, Yacatecuhtli, Yao
Z. Zababa, Zor, Zelus

Bibliography

Starr, Chester G. *A History of the Ancient World.* Oxford University Press. 1991

Sitchin, Zechariah. *The Stairway to Heaven.* Avon Books, NY 1980

The Savvy Convert's Guide to Choosing a Religion. Knock Knock, Venice, CA. 2008

Childress, David Hatcher. *Vimana Aircraft of Ancient India and Atlantis.* Adventures Unlimited Press, Illinois. 1991

Davis, Kenneth C. *Don't Know much About Mythology.* Harper Collins. NY, NY 2005

Cooke, Tim, Editor. *Concise History of World Religions.* National Geographic, Wash. DC. 2011

Hitchens, Christopher. *God is not Great.* Twelve Hatchette Book Group. USA. 2007

King, Ross. *Michelangelo and the Pope's Ceiling.* Penguin Books. 2002

Atlantis Rising Magazine

The New York Times

Wikipedia

Godchecker.com

Godfinder.org

Note for X: The sculpture has carved stylized Morning Glory tendrils. Flower buds of the *Hermia solicifolia* a member of the loosestrife family, produce auditory hallucinations, euphoria, general relaxation and improved memory.
Flowers of the *Rivea corymbosa,* and *Turbina corybosa.* Both in the morning glory family. Morning glory contains LSA which produces similar effects to LSD. Used by the Aztec, although large amounts of seeds produce mind-altering effects, they are highly toxic. Flowers of *Nicotiana rustica L.* Known as Picietl, related to tobacco. A wad of ground leaves mixed with lime was placed between the teeth and gums to give strength. Stylized caps of *Psilocybe aztecorum,* Tenonactl- 'Gods flesh' or 'Gods mushroom,' hallucinogenic mushroom. Fourteen species belonging to Psilocybe, Strophoria, and Conocybe families might also be employed.

Reviews: If you enjoyed this book, Michael P. Earney would appreciate it if you would leave a review on Amazon, Goodreads, or any other Review site you like.

Also, don't forget to tell your friends! Word of mouth advertising is the most precious *"Thank You"* a reader can ever give an author.

About the Author: Michael P. Earney is a fine arts painter who grew up in England. His writer's voice reflects curiosity and passion for the world of nature. His text is instructive yet playful. The illustrations are executed with grace and fine detail. Earney is in his element as artist, writer, educator, and naturalist. To learn more about this author's books and various achievements please visit his websites.

Contact Mr. Earney: themichaelearney@yahoo.com
Websites: www.MichaelEarney.com and www.EarneyWorks.com
Publisher: www.ErinGoBraghPublishing.com/authors/mearney

www.ingramcontent.com/pod-product-compliance
Lightning Source LLC
Chambersburg PA
CBHW051206220526
45473CB00003B/920